The
Ultimate Rip-Off:
A Taxing Tale

The Ultimate Rip-Off: A Taxing Tale is fiction and all the characters and adventures are imaginary. Any resemblance to actual persons living or dead is purely coincidental.

There hasn't been a member of Congress with a comprehensive understanding of the tax laws since Wilbur Mills, and I'm not a fan of Wilbur Mills.

—Stanford J. Schlesinger

Albert Einstein allegedly said that the hardest thing in the world to understand is the income tax.

Inflation is taxation without representation.

—Milton Friedman

Next to being shot at and missed, nothing is quite as satisfying as an income tax refund.

—F. J. Raymond

If you receive a tax refund you have loaned money to the federal government at an interest-free rate. Don't do it.

—D. Larry Crumbley

The
Ultimate Rip-Off:
A Taxing Tale

FIFTH EDITION

D. Larry Crumbley
Donald L. Ariail
Debra A. Salbador

CAROLINA ACADEMIC PRESS
Durham, North Carolina

Library of Congress Cataloging-in-Publication Data

Crumbley, D. Larry.
The ultimate rip-off : a taxing tale / D. Larry Crumbley...[et al.]. --
5th ed.
    p. cm.
ISBN 978-1-61163-135-7 (alk. paper)
1. Taxation--United States--Fiction. 2. Income tax--Fiction. I.
Title.

PS3553.R77U48 2012
813'.54--dc23

                                        2011036966

Cover photo credits:
blue jeans © Ulchik74/fotolia
hand and bills © WavebreakMediaMicro/fotolia
blank label patch © picsfive/fotolia

CAROLINA ACADEMIC PRESS
700 Kent Street
Durham, North Carolina 27701
Telephone (919) 489-7486
Fax (919) 493-5668
www.cap-press.com

Printed in the United States of America

Dedicated to Caleb, Daniel, Jacob, Ryan, Sloane, and Dane

Contents

Preface

The Ultimate Rip-Off is an exciting supplementary text for public finance, taxation, accounting, or tax research classes in a suspense thriller format. This instructional novel is ideal for an MBA program or law school, which has a light coverage of taxation or accounting. It can be used in IRS training programs for beginning agents or in a CPA firm's in-house training program.

Featuring sleuths who handle net worth statements and financial records the way most detectives handle guns, the humorous characters put taxation and forensic accounting concepts into real life individual and business decisions. Along the way, public financial concepts and political controversies, contemporary individual and corporate tax planning, tax fraud and avoidance, and the life of IRS employees are elucidated in a way both students and instructors will find gripping as well as informative. Never dull! This educational novel is both didactic and entertaining. So jump on board and enjoy a good read.

Mix fraud, crime, politics, and taxation together to get a better way of learning the taxation process. If used as a supplement to a taxation course or a public finance course, this gripping novel provides a painless way of learning many taxation principles. This suspenseful novel puts taxation and forensic concepts into words a novice can understand and enjoy. Jeff Burke, a Dirty Harry-type Special Agent in the IRS, goes beyond the law to find several rogues who are evading taxes.

I assumed my real name in a past edition. I adopted a pen name on earlier editions because a former department head told me not to write my first novel, because the novel would be an embarrassment to his university. Well, this is the fifth edition, and my first novel did not sink like the Titanic, being adopted at many universities and colleges. I have published twelve other educational novels, and I personally thank that department head for giving me the incentive to write more novels.

Comments and suggestions are welcomed. Thanks to the many students and faculty who have read and criticized the earlier editions. I appreciate many helpful comments and support from Sriharsha Atluri, Tony Billings, Nick Brignola, Tony Crumbley, Michael Davis, Brian Doherty, James Edwards, Ed Fenton, Dann Fisher, Tonya Flesher, Ron Flinn, Karyn Friske, Harold Goedde, Lenny Goodman, Jim Greenspan, Phil Harmelink, Jim Hasselback, Lester Heitger, Michael Licata, Howell Lynch, Joe Matoney, Ed Milan, Linda Nichols, Cherie O'Neil, Marilyn Phelan, Gene Seago, Stevenson Smith, Suresh Sonti, Carol Sullivan, and Len Weld. Of course, any errors are mine.

D. Larry Crumbley
Louisiana State University

Cast of Characters

Ted Abbott, a Harvard lawyer specializing in taxation, who represents Carl Strovee and Henry Silverman.

Nick Anderson, an elite Special Agent, who works for the Treasury Inspector General for the Tax Administration Division.

Tony Blake, a Revenue Agent in Scottsdale, Arizona.

Hank Brown, a Special Agent of the Criminal Investigation Division, who works closely with Jeff Burke.

Jeff Burke, a Special Agent of the Criminal Investigation Division of the IRS.

Jimmy Callaway, the Commissioner of the IRS.

Harry Cranford, Press Secretary of the President.

B.W. Flesher, the owner of Flesher Printing Company.

Rob Fowler, a suspected "runner" for the football-betting racket in Baltimore.

Rick Garrison, a police detective in Washington, D.C.

Ben Gibson, Attorney General of the United States.

Professor Gregory, Psychology Professor at the University of Kentucky.

Richard Onner, a computer expert working in the IRS National Computer Center in Martinsburg, West Virginia.

Jason Pabst, Nick Anderson's IRS supervisor.

Jack Rosenbaum, President of Rosenbaum, Inc., a rare coin business.

Charles Z. Samson, driver of the Sibbett Plumbing Outlet van.

Tish Scarbourg, the significant other of Richard Onner.

Henry Silverman, accountant who helped Carl Strovee cheat on his taxes.

Carl Strovee, a fraudulent psychic.

Debra Sweeney, a minister's wife in Pikeville, Kentucky.

Yvonne Talbert, a Revenue Agent.

Sam Westley, Jeff's supervisor.

The
Ultimate Rip-Off:
A Taxing Tale

Chapter 1

The mere fact that a taxpayer chooses one road in prefer-
ence to another, in order to avoid the hot sun of taxation,
is no reason to deny he actually traveled the first road.
—Hugh C. Bickford

Jeff Burke awoke on his side in pain. It was Monday, and he did
not wish to get up. But he had missed work on Friday, and Nick was
expecting him this morning.

Jeff liked to play softball—until Thursday. Jeff liked to pitch softball—until Thursday. Jeff was pitching in the top of the third inning.
One out, with a runner on first. His team was the Sentry Superstars.

The batter hit a sharp line drive, which struck the ground once
and then bounced wildly and hit Jeff directly in the groin area. Surprisingly Jeff picked up the softball and threw the runner out before collapsing and passing out.

One hour later he was resting in a bathtub of cold water with sore,
swollen plumbing. On Friday morning he was sitting in the doctor's
office. The office was filled with old people. What has Medicare
done—made the doctor's office a retreat of the "old fogies?" Jeff did
notice the pretty, blondish woman with an overworked look leave
the office about 20 minutes into his long wait. Other than that event,
the only stimulating items in the office were magazines, all of which
were three to four months old. He tried to read some stories in *People,* but he could not keep his mind focused on the words.

Two hours he had to wait. Then one minute with the doctor with
a sullen, narrow face. Jeff winced when the fat, nimble hands explored
his swollen private parts. The doctor mumbled, "You're lucky to
have anything left. Wear jocks and keep an ice pack on them."

"Just great," Jeff thought. "An ice pack on my testicles!" Jeff made a mental note to have the doctor audited as he left the doctor's office. Jeff worked for the IRS, and he knew that many medical doctors earn a high income. A doctor might keep vital income records personally in order to avoid letting employees know about his or her business. Some doctors have a constant turnover of clerical help to accomplish the same result. Thus, fees may be collected without the employees' knowledge and omitted from the doctor's records. A nice way of avoiding taxes.

"Wonder how he invests his money?" Jeff thought. Jeff recalled that the IRS Audit Guide indicated that many doctors are active investors in securities, bonds, rental properties, oil properties, and especially real estate. The Audit Guide was, of course, the "bible" of a good agent. If he gives prescriptions for the druggist next door, I bet he has a kickback arrangement with the druggist.

The Audit Guide indicates that doctors often have kickback arrangements with druggists on prescriptions, with opticians on prescriptions for glasses and frames, or with specialists on referrals. "I wish I could destroy his golden goose," Jeff mumbled to himself as he slowly maneuvered down several stone steps. A plump, smooth-faced woman leading a snotty little kid into the doctor's office gave him a bitter look. Of course, he knew he could not audit the doctor, but at least he could dream of the good old days. Today, an agent can look at only the taxpayers' files that they are auditing. Tax returns with the highest examination potential are sent to the local examination groups on the basis of workload capacities.

The sky was overcast and looked as if it might snow. "Great," Jeff thought. "All I need is to have to walk on ice and snow in this condition." His breath misted in front of him as he walked slowly toward his parked car. Jeff somehow maneuvered his body into his dirty car and drove toward his apartment. He stopped at a pharmacy and purchased two jock straps.

* * *

Jeff slowly got out of bed. He had slept badly during the night. Each time he moved, he ached. He gingerly tucked his sore organs into his jock support, thinking he was possibly lucky he'd broken up with his delightful girlfriend, Shirley, because he could forget about a sex life for a while. The split-up had been extremely painful to Jeff.

Jeff was a Special Agent in the Baltimore Office. Criminal violations of the Internal Revenue Code are the responsibilities of Special Agents of the Criminal Investigation Division (CID). The Intelligence Division of the IRS had its beginning on July 1, 1919, as the brainchild of Daniel C. Roper, the Commissioner of the then Internal Revenue. These silent investigators have caught many tax evaders as well as put many top criminals in prison. Such notorious organized crime figures as Al "Scarface" Capone, Frank Costello, Waxey Gordon, Bernard Goldfine, and Johnny Torrio (the father of modem gangsterdom) were sent to prison by the work of Special Agents.

While many give credit to FBI agent Eliot Ness for sending the notorious mobster, Al Capone, to prison, it was the meticulous forensic accounting work of special agent Frank Wilson of the IRS (then called the U.S. Bureau of Internal Revenue) that actually built the tax case against Al Capone.

The IRS, not the FBI, toppled the empires of such political bosses as Huey Long of Louisiana, "Nucky" Johnson of Atlantic City, and Tom Pendergast of Kansas City. IRS personnel were some of the first forensic accountants in the U.S.

He had been a Revenue Agent before asking for a transfer. The main federal snooper in the tax force is the Revenue Agent. A Revenue Agent provides a routine examination of taxpayers. A Special Agent is called into action when fraud is suspected by a Revenue Agent, or when local and state police officers make a "drug bust."

He remembered the tone in Nick's voice Thursday. "Jeff," Nick had said, "I believe we have a crooked IRS agent in a critical position. There are probably other taxpayers involved in this fraud, so I need your help." Jeff knew that Special Agents investigate taxpayers, not other agents. No other information was given, and Jeff had made an appointment to see Nick at 10:00 a.m. Monday in Washington.

Jeff had known Nick at Penn State. Both had earned their degrees in accounting in "Happy Valley." Penn State is located in State College, Pennsylvania, and it is equally inaccessible from most parts of Pennsylvania. "Happy Valley" probably originated because there is absolutely nothing to do except study and go to bed with your spouse — assuming you could find one.

During their junior year at Penn State, Nick and Jeff had often double-dated. Jeff's girlfriend, Jane, had been a pleasantly plump brunette — chubby but cuddly. In between football games and dorm room necking sessions, Jeff had learned some psychology, since Jane's major had been psychology.

Nick Anderson started out as a strike-force agent. Sometimes called "bird-dog" agents, their so-called strike-force investigations often resulted in fraud charges. Although "bird-dog" agents are regular Revenue Agents, their basic function was to uncover possible criminal activities. They work closely with other federal, state, and local law enforcement agencies, but at all times control of the investigation is under the authority of the Commissioner of the IRS or delegate.

Strike-force agents have been known to work undercover, close to the criminal activities. They hang around racetracks and gambling casinos. They pose as gamblers, pimps, dope peddlers, elevator doormen, and any other position that will uncover hidden revenues. They may tap telephone conversations or open people's mail. They look for "juice." "Juice" is the slang for revenue from taxpayers. Revenue is the lifeblood of the IRS and the federal government.

One strike force, code-named "Operation Bird-Dog," descended upon the Ali-Quarry fight in Atlanta in 1970. These agents recorded the license tag numbers of the ringsiders. A number of expensive, custom-built cars turned up on the list. These lists were then forwarded to IRS officials around the United States, and the owners' income tax forms were audited.

IRS files indicated that the roaring Twenties had seemingly returned to Atlanta. The styles of the Twenties prevailed with the males challenging the females for the extreme in dress and brilliance of color, wearing wide-brimmed hats, double-breasted jackets, two piece suits with coats to the knees. Some wore full-length minks.

However, in 1998, Congress prohibited financial status or economic reality techniques to determine the existence of unreported income unless an agent has a reasonable indication that there is a likelihood of unreported income. A revenue agent may drive by a taxpayer's home and conduct a LexisNexis search to determine whether a person purchased real estate during the year without violating the statutory prohibition against financial status audits.

These restrictions may be the reason for the so-called tax gap or underground economy. The IRS estimates that annual noncompliance is approximately 16 percent of revenue or a whopping $354 billion, before collecting $55 billion through enforcement. Agents believe that they have to audit with their hands tied behind their backs. A recent survey found that 13 percent of taxpayers felt that it was acceptable to cheat a little when filing income taxes, up from 9 percent in 2008.

Nick was now a member of a little-known, elite group of agents, called Special Agents who work for the Treasury Inspector General for Tax Administration Division. Their targets were dishonest Treasury Department employees, as well as government officials and employees. After Lewinskygate, Whitewater, Travelgate, Watergate, Iranscam, Richard Nixon's backdated gift, Congressman Wayne Hays' Waterloo with the sex-payroll affair, and the confirmation of Lyndon Johnson's two hundred-vote fraud, a special unit was established to look into the conduct of any government official.

Before he resigned, Nixon got into trouble with his taxes. Lyndon Johnson and other politicians had donated their personal letters and papers to charitable organizations. They took sizable charitable deductions based upon the fair market value of the donations. With a Republican president in office, the Democratic Congress changed the rules to allow a deduction only for the actual cost of the paper or letterhead. Nixon tried to beat the effective date of the new law change and donated his vice-presidential papers to the National Archives. Critics asserted that Nixon's lawyer backdated the deed transferring the papers.

Later, in the election campaign between Jimmy Carter and Gerald Ford, Carter made taxation reform one of his major campaign issues. Then, within his first year in office, Carter showed an insignificant tax liability on his tax return. A large investment tax credit from the purchase of peanut machinery reduced his tax burden. An astute politician, Carter made political hay by "donating" $6,000 to the IRS. His reasoning was that everyone should pay *some* taxes. A comedian during this time wondered out loud how you could trust someone who volunteers to pay extra taxes with a smile.

Nick was a TIGTA Special Agent. If Nick had found fraud by an employee, he would need a Special Agent to follow up any fraud with outside taxpayers. Jeff figured that Nick needed his help in the taxpayer investigation. Once fraud is discovered by a Revenue Agent, he should suspend his activities at the earliest opportunity without disclosing to the taxpayer the reason for the suspension. The agent, however, should take the necessary steps to determine that there is fraud before asking for a Special Agent.

At 9:45 a.m., Jeff was slowly making his way toward the main entrance at 1111 Constitution Avenue. He had made reasonable time coming from Baltimore to Washington. Three arches rose two stories to the architrave. The seven-story concrete, limestone and marble structure was the IRS's national office building. It was in the Federal Triangle complex of government buildings in Washington, D.C. Built in 1930 at a cost of ten million dollars, its design was inspired by the Somerset House on London's Strand — the structure that housed Britain's tax collection agency. The British agency was previously called Inland Revenue, but its name was changed in 2005 to HM Revenue and Customs. How soon they forget, Jeff thought, recalling the Boston tea party.

Jeff signed in with the guard and walked through the security machine. With the high crime rate in D.C. and the possibility of a certified lunatic or terrorist bringing a bomb into the federal buildings, all federal buildings had armed guards at the entrances.

Jeff entered a vacant elevator and jabbed the button for the fourth floor. He saw a reflection of his windblown, short hair and brown mustache on the shiny, smooth wall of the elevator. He wore stylish photo-reactive lenses, so his lenses were still dark. He liked glasses because they offered protection, and he thought they made him look younger and more intelligent. He smiled back as he patted his hair down. When the elevator jerked to a stop, he walked down the hall to Nick's office.

As an Inspector, bespectacled, pipe-smoking Nick seemed to enjoy involvement in criminal investigations and repeatedly became involved in cases which ultimately were referred to a Special Agent. That's probably why he was placed on the bird-dog squad.

Nick looked up from his computer console. "Hello, Jeff. How are you?" With a fussy movement he removed his wireframed glasses.

"Terrible," nodded Jeff. "Got hit in the family jewels Thursday night with a softball."

"Bad on the sex life, isn't it?" smiled Nick. "How's your softball team doing?"

"Lousy. We've won about half our games. We need more hitting. What do you have for me today?"

"I may have another hot one for you," replied Nick. "Have a seat."

Jeff settled into a straight-back chair.

Nick gulped a swallow of coffee from a styrofoam cup and gestured with his pencil toward the folder in front of him. On the left side of his desk was the Service's standard personal computer. They had been introduced in the late nineties.

"Richard Onner is our target," Nick said crisply. "He is a computer expert working in our National Computer Center in Martinsburg, West Virginia." He replaced his glasses on his hawk-like nose.

After a short pause, Nick continued. "We received an anonymous tip about Richard approximately a year and a half ago that he was living beyond his means. The anonymous letter indicated that he was probably taking bribes."

Jeff recalled that few taxpayers knew about the IRS's formal informer's program. But rewards range from 15% to 30% of the taxes and penalties collected by the IRS, exceeding $2 million, as a result of tips. Agents affectionately call such rewards a "fink fee." Ex-wives or husbands, jilted girlfriends, and disgruntled friends and neighbors create approximately 12,000 tips per year. The IRS even has a tip hot line (1-800-829-0433), and the appropriate form to file is Form 3949A, where the amount in dispute less the reward is still discretionary with the IRS, up to 30%.

One of the most famous cases involved an oral surgeon's nurse who informed the Special Agent's office in Los Angeles that her employer-dentist was keeping two sets of books. While the dentist went on vacation, the agents arrived for their investigation.

With the cooperation of the nurse, a dozen Special Agents examined more than twenty thousand patients' charts in order to determine the dentist's true income. The nurse then helped obtain a confession from the dentist.

Our heroine was not rewarded for her "good deed." The nurse was blacklisted by the medical and dental professions in the area. She was unable to find similar employment and had to leave the city.

Another famous anonymous tip from a businessman in New York involved Virginia Hill, a woman who was "involved" with organized crime. She shocked the Kefauver Committee by attributing her wealth to the fact that she was "the world's best lay." Congress initiated a probe of Virginia's role in organized crime, and she eventually died after swallowing twenty-eight sleeping pills in March 1966.

An informer must, of course, ask for the reward. A reward will not be given automatically. A Form 211, Application for Reward for Original Information, must be filed with the whistleblower office of the IRS. Payment is made under IRC Section 7623(a) at the discretion of the IRS. Approximately one of every six claims is approved. Of course, the informer normally remains anonymous from the person he or she is reporting. Then the informer has to pay taxes on the fink fee. The IRS carefully checks their tax returns in the subsequent tax year.

The mother lode of whistleblowing awards occurred in 2011, when an accountant squealed on his employer who was not paying his "fair share of taxes." The accountant received an award of $4.5 million, but only after he hired a lawyer to push the issue when the IRS formal whistleblower office was slow to pay.

Jeff had about twenty unpaid informants. The confidentiality of an informant must always be protected. Even if ordered to reveal the identity of an informant in court under the threat of a contempt citation, the IRS agent should remain silent.

Only his manager knew the identity of Jeff's informants. The informant's names were listed on a three-by-five-inch index card in a sealed envelope. The envelope was to be opened by his Section Chief only if Jeff were missing or in personal danger.

Informants have been known to break laws to obtain information. Jeff had paid an informant $7,000 recently to obtain tax information about some Bahamian corporations. The informant had photocopied the contents of the official's briefcase while he was entertained by a woman obtained by the IRS informant. The information had been quite damaging to the taxpayer's tax battle with the IRS.

In the past Jeff had used several female informants to learn about the sex lives of several prominent businessmen. Using an informant to "bug" a possible tax evader was not uncommon. The "bugging of the Democratic headquarters" in the Watergate complex was not an isolated incident. Had not "landslide Lyndon" bugged Goldwater during their political campaign? Johnson and Kennedy had tapped on a wholesale basis.

Jeff asked, "Who is the informant?"

Nick smiled owlishly, "We don't know who the squeal letter is from; however, the handwriting and perfumed paper would seem to indicate that the squealer is a woman. Probably an ex-girlfriend."

"At first I thought the charge had no substance. However, I talked to Onner's security broker and his banks and examined the records of his transactions. I'm convinced he is not reporting all of his income. But I don't know from whom he receives the income, or how he receives it, or why."

"He has gambled away about $18,000 over the past year and has spent about $20,000 on his current girlfriend."

"I used the net worth analysis on him, and he is not reporting about $33,000 of income. Here, look for yourself." Nick's eyes were bright with excitement as he handed a computer printout to Jeff. On the computer sheet was the following:

Confidential — Net Worth Analysis
IRS Personnel
Richard Onner 241-56-7682

Net Worth (end of year)	$149,000
Net Worth (beginning of year)	−102,000
	$ 47,000
Nondeductible expenditures	+ 48,000
Reconstructed income	$ 95,000
Reported income	− 62,000
Unreported income	$ 33,000

Jeff knew immediately that this information was damaging. The indirect net worth method was upheld by the Supreme Court in 1954 in *Holland v. U.S.* as a valid method of gathering evidence for conviction of tax evasion. This technique can be used when there is a year-to-year increase in net worth and a taxpayer does not have adequate records to determine taxable income or fraud is suspected. Of course, the tough part of the net worth analysis is determining a taxpayer's yearly expenditures.

Jeff looked up and responded, "Do you have any ideas of his possible sources of income?"

"Nope. He has no wealthy family members so nontaxable gifts or an inheritance are out of the question. He drives a Porsche and spends money as if it's going out of style. He must be involved with some other taxpayers. That's why I need your help."

"I have not contacted Onner, so he is unaware of the fact that he is being investigated. Of course, I must prepare a report, which goes directly to the Commissioner's office since we are dealing with such a sensitive individual. I plan to send the letter tomorrow. I have told no one else."

Jeff looked at his watch and then said, "Okay, I'll check him out. You file your report with the Commissioner, but let's keep it under wraps. There may be a simple explanation, so we don't want to damage Onner's reputation with false charges. Keep me informed as to any other developments. I'll drive out to Martinsburg tomorrow." However, Jeff knew that once an IRS agent had embarked on an indirect, time-consuming method of computing income of a taxpayer, he did not wish to waste such efforts. Some tax revenues must result from such efforts, or he would receive criticism from his supervisor.

"Have you made an extra copy of Onner's tax returns?" Jeff asked, knowing the answer already and wondering why he had even bothered to ask.

"You bet," responded Nick, handing a file to Jeff. A phone started ringing in the next office.

Jeff rose to leave. As he turned and left, he was thinking about how efficient Nick was. The phone was still ringing as he passed the door to the next office. Nick was finishing the letter to the Commissioner outlining the suspicious facts concerning Richard Onner before Jeff made his way slowly out of the elevator into the sunlight.

He had his work cut out for him. As he was contemplating his next step, he realized that it also was time for him to file Form 5043, Criminal Investigation Monthly Activity Report, which must be prepared by all criminal investigation special agents.

Chapter 2

You can have a lord, you can have a king, but the man to fear is the tax collector.
—Ancient Iraqi Proverb

The radio was on and a soft tune filled the room. Carl liked to work with the background of a radio. He did not consciously hear the news reporter begin the hourly report, but Carl looked up from the sheaf of paper in front of him when he heard his name mentioned.

"Folks, here are the latest predictions of Carl Strovee –

"Madonna shall divorce for the third time and wed David Letterman.

"David Eisenhower will beat Joseph Kennedy III in the New Hampshire primary.

"The Houston Astros will win the World Series.

"New Zealand will win the America's Cup a second time."

Carl thought about a cigarette but instead leaned back in his chair. "Rats!" Carl exclaimed to himself. "How can I work on predictions with the IRS on my back?"

The letter had arrived yesterday addressed to Carl Strover; they had even misspelled his name! Millions had heard of Strovee the Swami through his books and newspaper columns on astrology. This would be the second year in a row they had audited his return.

Carl had first gained prominence when he accurately predicted the date—within two days—of Iraq's invasion of Kuwait. In fact, many of his predictions had been accurate. He had predicted that President Obama would be elected president, that Dr. Rand Paul would win a Senate seat, and that Kevin Costner would win an Oscar, even after *Waterworld* and *The Postman* disasters.

The letter indicated that Agent Yvonne Talbert had arranged for an office audit of Carl's last two tax returns. "Please bring the document or minutes that show that the stock you sold was Section 1244 stock," the letter had stated. Carl had claimed a $50,000 ordinary deduction and a $3,000 capital loss on his tax return for the sale of small business stock.

Carl thought, "How much money have I hidden from the government? Doesn't everyone cheat on their income taxes?" August 15th, 3:00 p.m., at the Federal Building, Room 2001 was the information in the letter. Two days before his birthday. A great birthday present! Carl would be 35. He was still single.

And Henry had not been in town yesterday. Henry Silverman, his accountant, had helped Carl set up a system of hiding about thirty percent of his gross receipts.

"Simple," he had said. "Many of the receipts that you receive are cash payments. When you prepare a personal horoscope for a client, he pays you with a check or with cash. Many clients do not wish anyone to know they deal with an astrologer."

"We'll keep two sets of books," Henry had said. "One set is for the IRS and the other set is for your personal benefit. Remember, most of the payments received from your clients are not deductible by them, so they will not keep a record of their payments. Also, the top 50 percent of taxpayers like you and I pay more than 97 percent of federal income taxes. The bottom 50 percent of taxpayers pay less than 3 percent. Our lawmakers should expand the tax base. Those poorer people should pay more—not just get welfare in the form of the earned income credit."

"Gee, I'm in the 39.6% tax bracket already," Carl reflected. "What more do they want? Even hiding 30% of my cash receipts, I'm still paying about 25 cents out of each $1 to pay for the lousy government welfare programs." Henry had given Carl a copy of *Take It Off!*, published by no less than Playboy Press, which provided more than 1,000 tax deductions that most people overlook. Had Ralph Nader not predicted that the average taxpayer works more than three months out of the year for the government? "In the 35% tax bracket, I work almost four months out of the year for the federal government," Carl thought.

Carl smiled gently as he thought. "Ironic. Much of my work is fraud, and I'm systematically cheating the IRS. How do I make predictions? Some of it is luck, but most of it is merely reading everything. My nearly photographic mind allows me to put together various pieces of information into believable predictions. But much of my success is guaranteed by making enough predictions so that some of them come true."

"Thank goodness people are forgetful. They don't remember that I predicted that George Bush would not run for re-election, the Great Salt Lake would dry up, there would be a depression in 1999, and an earthquake would make Chappaquiddick Island disappear. Where was my mind when I made those turkeys?" He sipped some wine from a glass on his table.

Henry's telephone service had indicated that he would be back around 10:00 a.m. today. "Better call him," Carl spoke to himself as he turned down the radio. He was fuming with impatience. "I surely hope he is in, and I don't have to speak to that blasted recording again. I'm always tempted to shout obscenities into the phone and leave the number of the local police department." He dialed the number again.

"Hello, are you paying too much in taxes?" was the pleasant response at the other end of the line. "We can show you how better records and some planning can save you money."

"Yes, this is Carl Strovee. Could I speak to Henry?" Carl spoke in a high, almost soprano voice.

"Just a moment, Mr. Strovee," the sweet female voice said.

Each time Carl called and received Henry's standard question— "Are you paying too much in taxes?"—he was always impressed that Henry did not miss a chance to advertise his trade.

"Hello, Carl, this is Henry. What scheme do you wish to try this week?" Henry asked in a low, polite voice.

"How to beat an IRS audit."

"What?" was Henry's puzzled response.

"They're auditing me again. I got a letter yesterday. They want to see information about the Section 1244 stock. You know, from my corporation that went bankrupt. I got mostly an ordinary loss rather than just a capital loss."

"Now don't panic, Carl. Everything went smoothly last year, didn't it? You didn't even have to attend the conference. It's probably just a routine audit. How many times have you been audited?"

"Three times."

"Three years in a row?"

"No, they skipped one year," replied Carl.

"I thought so. They normally don't audit anyone more than two years in a row if no adjustments are made, although they can examine up to the last three years' returns on any one audit."

"Let me read you the list of things they want."

"Why don't you just bring the letter in around five o'clock this afternoon. That will give me a chance to review your file."

"Good-bye," responded Carl at about the same time that there was a dull click at the other end of the line. Henry put down the phone, frustrated. He clenched his fist and softly pounded the desk with it. His calculator rattled on his desk. Henry certainly did not appreciate this unpleasant news. Carl Strovee was vulnerable. "How much was he ripping off from the government?" Henry wondered. "About thirty percent. Trouble. Hopefully it is just a routine audit."

Henry Silverman was not a certified public accountant. He was a tax preparer. He had dropped out of City College after he had taken enough courses to sit for the CPA exam. He sat for the CPA exam several times, but he could not seem to pass it. Why does an accountant need to know about calculus, linear programming, and the rest of that junk? Then they passed a requirement that you had to have a college degree to sit for the examination, so Henry gave up on the CPA examination. Not that Henry was dumb. He had a sound knowledge of accounting, especially tax accounting. But he did not have the capstone—the CPA certificate.

The CPA certificate was the cream of the crop. It was the dream of every accountant. The exam was tough. Only about 40% of candidates pass the entire exam on their first sitting. The two day exam of accounting, auditing, taxation, and other sophisticated matters, became a computerized exam in 2004. Now the exam can be taken in parts, which makes it easier. The certificate is the union card to work with one of the large CPA firms. In the late '70s the Metcalf Report indicated that the then six biggest accounting firms had a "stranglehold on the profession and obligingly twisted accounting principles to suit their corporate clients." Most accountants heatedly denied these charges. With the disappearance of Arthur Andersen and accounting firms mergers, there was now the "Big Four."

The accounting profession is different than the legal profession. Whereas, the legal profession is made up of smaller firms with many small practitioners, the accounting profession is dominated by four large CPA firms that have branch offices in most major cities and affiliate firms around the world.

Henry had not worked with a "big-four firm." They would not hire anyone without an accounting degree. He had worked with a smaller firm in New York City. He had been lucky even to be hired by a small firm. His uncle got him the job, somehow.

Henry soon quit the small CPA firm in New York when it became evident that he would not pass the CPA exam, and therefore, had no hope of ever moving up in the firm. He went to Washington, D.C. and set up his own shop without a union card.

He was lucky he did not have his CPA in the early days. He had survived by advertising. In those early days a CPA could not advertise. It was against their Code of Ethics. Actually it was a way of preserving their caste system.

But Henry had advertised and advertised. He was able to find bookkeeping work, referred to by accountants as write-up work, and eat. Write-up work was the scorn of CPAs in international accounting firms. Write-up work was demeaning and difficult. But someone had to keep the detailed records for small and medium-sized companies. Just as armies travel on their stomachs, industries would grind to a halt without recordkeeping.

Henry knew he was intelligent because he had passed the Treasury examination while in New York and became an enrolled agent— an EA. A CPA or lawyer is automatically admitted to practice before the Treasury Department. Other persons have to take and pass a difficult examination which is given annually. Passing the exam requires detailed tax knowledge. Henry passed the exam on the first try. Henry liked taxation.

Being admitted to practice before the Treasury Department had been a problem when he moved to Washington. A person admitted to practice is prohibited from using any title such as tax accountant or from advertising in any fashion. In effect, true tax experts were not allowed to advertise, whereas the unscrupulous tax "experts" were allowed to advertise their wares. Thus, he had to drop his status as an EA when he moved to Washington. He had to advertise in order to eat.

Advertising had been helpful to Henry in the beginning. Two events moved him into his present consulting firm. First, early in 1977, the Supreme Court gave lawyers the right to advertise. Within a short time CPAs began to advertise. Now it is not uncommon to see full-page ads in the *Wall Street Journal, Barrons,* and other publications extolling the virtues of this or that CPA firm.

Second, with the increasing use of computers in tax and accounting work, Henry's prospects had dimmed. In desperation, Henry began to advise clients about various shaky and shady techniques. He suggested techniques that did not appear in *Accountant's News* and *Tax Tricks and Techniques.* Henry began to advocate fraud.

Every "red-blooded accountant" knows the classic verbiage of Judge Learned Hand, a famous tax judge:

> Over and over again courts have said that there is nothing sinister in arranging one's affairs so as to keep taxes as low as possible. Everybody does so, rich or poor; and all do right, for nobody owes any public duty to pay more than the law demands: taxes are enforced extractions, not voluntary contributions. To demand more in the name of morals is mere cant.

Henry's techniques went beyond the fine line between tax avoidance versus tax evasion. Tax avoidance is fine under the law, but tax
evasion may result in free room and board in a federal penitentiary.

Henry knew that any attempt to avoid taxes was not necessarily
a criminal offense. Attempts to avoid, reduce, minimize, or allevi-
ate taxes by legitimate means are permissible. Anyone who avoids
taxes does not misrepresent or conceal. Such a taxpayer merely
shapes events to reduce, defer, or eliminate his tax liability. Upon
the happening of events, the taxpayer makes a full disclosure. For
example, the creation of a bona fide partnership in order to divide
the income among several individual partners is okay. Tax representatives can be advocates for clients, taking reasonable and sup-
portive positions.

On the other hand, Henry was aware that evasion involves subterfuge, deceit, camouflage, or concealment in order to color or ob-
scure events. A taxpayer may not make things seem other than they
are. The willful attempt in any manner to evade or defeat a tax con-
stitutes a criminal offense — a fine of not more than $250,000
($500,000 for a corporation) plus court costs or imprisonment of not
more than five years, or both. The three elements of the crime of tax
evasion are willfulness, an attempt to evade tax, and additional tax
due. A tax representative who helps a taxpayer evade taxes is guilty
of tax preparer fraud and subject to severe legal consequences.

Henry was an excellent speaker. He now traveled a great deal
giving unadvertised seminars on tax fraud techniques to high-tax
bracket taxpayers. His fee was steep; each individual had to pay
$1,200 for his eight-hour seminar. But his advice was worth it. As
the Internal Revenue Code became more and more complicated,
more people signed up for his seminar. Former Senator Sam Nunn
described the tax code as "thousands of pages of pet rocks that had
nothing to do with the national interest."

His most profitable flim-flam was advising taxpayers how to set
up their own church. Such a scheme can relieve a taxpayer of the
federal income tax, the state franchise tax, and local taxes. An individual can become a minister for $30 and can even purchase for
a fifty dollar "offering" a mail-order Honorary Doctor of Divinity

certificate from the American Fellowship Church. For an offering of $10 per month for recordkeeping purposes, this same organization will send a Church Charter and tax-exempt status.

The taxpayer can appoint his wife and daughter to be the church secretary and treasurer. Then the taxpayer can put his $20,000 paychecks (less approximately $3,200 of federal taxes) into a church fund recorded by the church treasurer. Next the church can buy or rent a house for their minister to live in. Estimate about $4,000 a year for this amount. Our minister is entitled to a living allowance for himself and his family. Estimate another $9,000. Add $3,000 for phone, utilities, and insurance. The minister will need a car to perform church work. This car can be used for personal work. Approximately $3,000. At the end of the year, our taxpayer can apply for a refund of the $3,200 withheld. Thus, his entire salary is tax-free. Henry knew that this religious tax shelter was as porous as a leaky boat.

Another technique that Henry advocated was setting up an apocalypse trust. A trust is a special entity established by an individual with someone called the trustee in charge of operations of the special entity. Under this apocalypse arrangement, a taxpayer transfers to a trust all of his assets and assigns his lifetime services to the trust. For example, a dentist might transfer his place of business to a trust. The beneficiaries are generally the taxpayer's family, with the grantor retaining broad powers over the income and principal of the trust. The trust collects all of the taxpayer's income and deducts all of the taxpayer's expenses. The purpose of this arrangement is to shift income to taxpayers in lower tax brackets as well as to avoid the estate tax. Obviously the IRS was opposed to such an arrangement, but such opposition did not stop taxpayers from trying it. Henry knew this was another leaky tax shelter, but it pulled in the bucks for him.

Henry recalled that a Florida tax return preparer filed an amended federal income tax return for *Blade II* star Wesley Snipes requesting a $7.3 million refund for taxes paid in 1997, maintaining that the actor had no foreign taxable income that year. The refund request was based on the notion that only foreign income is subject to U.S. taxation. Published reports estimated Snipes' earnings to be around $18 million.

Snipes told shock talk show host Howard Stern that he was merely a bystander, and "I pay all my taxes." Snipes did not get a refund. In November 2010, Snipes was ordered to start serving a three-year prison sentence for failing to file tax returns.

The Australia Taxation Office accused actor Paul Hogan, star of the "Crocodile Dundee" movies of misrepresenting his tax residency status to the U.S. and Australia. He and his tax advisor, Tony Stewart, allegedly engaged in a scheme or conspiracy to allow money to be paid to Hogan when he was not a tax resident of any country, and therefore the payments were free of taxes. So Mick "Crocodile Dundee" tried to be a man without a country to avoid taxation.

Henry did have one characteristic of an accountant. Although he was black and had a neatly trimmed black mustache, he was conservative. He subscribed to such newsletters as *The Duff Times, Inflation Survival Letter, and Mick's World Currency Report*. He had been the one who introduced the scheme to avoid taxation using the standard gold content of the dollar. He encouraged several individuals to file their Form 1040 but pay no taxes. They then asserted that they were not required to pay taxes because the symbol "$" means "dollars," and its meaning for purpose of the tax law is the same as for the law describing the content of the dollar. The taxpayers maintained that they received no such "dollars." In essence, the taxpayers argued that a dollar is not a dollar because its purchasing power had declined and because paper currency cannot be converted into gold. Henry's idea lost in court.

This type of scheme did lead Henry into his latest venture. He was publishing a private newsletter informing his readers how to evade taxes. The annual subscription cost for "How to Cheat and Defraud the IRS" was $900. He published it under a pseudonym, I. M. Clever.

The need for the pseudonym was obvious. Henry had once been arrested on an indictment alleging a violation of federal income tax laws. He had been accused of knowingly preparing a false letter in connection with a tax matter. He had beaten the rap, but it paid to be cautious when dealing with the IRS.

Henry had read several weeks ago about 26 Bronx and Manhattan tax preparers who used dead people to claim about $95 million in tax refunds for clients. Maybe he could make a movie called *Tax Returns of the Living Dead*. Probably wouldn't sell. But would it be a tax shelter?

Henry frowned, irritated by the call from Carl. He returned to the incomplete partnership return in front of him. He was working on the Schedule K items. With double taxation of corporate income, the flow-through type entities had multiplied over the years, and the IRS audits only about one out of 400 partnership tax returns. Thus, the partnership vehicle is an efficient entity for tax cheaters when used in layers. Sitting on Henry's untidy desk was his dog-eared copy from *Taxes—The Tax Magazine* of an article entitled "Dealing with the 'Authorities:' Determining Valid Legal Authority In Advising Clients, Rendering Opinions, Preparing Tax Returns and Avoiding Penalties."

Chapter 3

Most voters would rather have their purse or wallet stolen then be audited by the IRS.

— Frank Luntz

Martinsburg, West Virginia, is about seventy miles west of Washington. Located at the head of the Shenandoah Valley, this city houses the National Computer Center of the IRS. The "Martinsburg Monster" is the nickname of the enormous IBM computers in a multistory brick and glass structure. These high-speed electronic digital computers have more than a thousand miles of master tapes, which contain the tax records of all U.S. taxpayers for the past three years.

Opened officially in 1961, this computer complex is the heart of the IRS's tax administration. A taxpayer files his return with his regional service center. A scanning machine feeds the data from the return into a computer and records such information on a magnetic tape. Uncle Sam collects about $2.3 trillion in taxes from tax returns each year. About 45 percent comes from individual income taxes, 36 percent from payroll taxes, and 12 percent from corporate income taxes.

These magnetic tapes are sent to the National Computer Center. Each reel contains about 15,000 tax returns. At the Center, the information is posted by a computer to each taxpayer's master file. The master file includes data about the taxpayer for a three-year period. The master files are kept up to date through weekly updating. The tax return tapes and the output tapes prepared at the Center are returned to the various regional centers.

Within two years, a taxpayer's return is matched with Form 1099s and W-2s coming from employers, banks, and so forth. If the return does not match with the other documents, the return is sent to the appropriate service center to be visually inspected. If missing, a CP 2000 notice is generated, and the taxpayer will get a "friendly" letter. The computer also checks to see whether deductions, interest, dividend income, royalties, and other items fall within normal ranges. A discriminant income function (DIF) picks certain tax returns, which have the greatest likelihood of error, cheating, and potential tax deficiency. There is always a chance that the return will be audited. In fact, less than 1% of all tax returns are audited. The more complicated a return and the higher the taxable income, the greater the chance of an audit.

A taxpayer compliance measurement project called the National Research Program (NRP) is designed to extract data from a stratified sample of 50,000 regular taxpayer audits. Randomly selected taxpayers come from 30 audit classes to improve the discriminant income function (DIF) used to select taxpayers for audit. About 2,000 of these taxpayers are subject to line-by-line audits, once called the Taxpayer Compliance Measurement Program (TCMP), the results of which are used to "fine tune" the DIF program.

The IRS has struggled with a computer modernization program that has misused or wasted more than $400 million since 1986. The systems are a mess with nine separate unconnected databases. It takes about 10 days for updated information in the master files to appear on the computer screens of IRS agents in the field.

Richard Onner was employed as a computer operator at the National Service Center. He was a competent employee. In fact, he was downright cocky about his computer ability. He had worked at the Center for five years, but knew he had probably reached the extent of his advancement within the IRS.

Richard was divorced. His first marriage had ended because he liked to run around. His first mistake was now costing him $1,000 per month in alimony payments. "But at least it's a deduction for adjusted gross income," Richard rationalized.

Richard thought of himself as a Don Juan or maybe a young Robert Redford. He was currently living with Tish Scarbourg. She had a gift of gab but no sense of reality. She was attractive.

Richard and Tish were lying in bed relaxing.

"When can we get married?"

Richard turned over and noticed his tanned body in the mirrors on the ceiling. Tish bounced up and down as the water in the waterbed settled back. "You really know when to hit a man."

"Well, this is the only time I can get your undivided attention. Between computers, hang gliding, and coins ..." She didn't finish the sentence.

Richard tried to stifle a yawn. "How much money do you earn at the advertising agency?"

"What?"

"How much money do you earn per year?"

"What's that got to do with marriage?"

"Just answer the question."

"About $49,000," Tish replied in a loud voice. "You should know, you spend part of it."

"If we get married, we'll have to pay more taxes. There are marriage penalties."

"You're kidding me."

"Nope. Our more enlightened society *and* the sometimes puritanical tax laws no longer frown upon cohabitation—uh, living together. Where two individuals have comparable incomes, they pay less taxes by living together without marriage. We can enjoy the blessing of love while minimizing our contributions to the federal government."

"Please talk in simple language."

"If we get married, you and I will have to pay more taxes. We are better off filing separate tax returns. Marriage will force us into higher tax brackets. Plus, our married filing jointly standard deduction will be less, our total alternative minimum taxable income exemptions would be less ..."

Tish snapped, "What a heck of an argument against marriage, especially after I gave you such a good time." She turned over, a trifle peeved.

Richard did not mention one advantage of marriage. The IRS generally cannot obtain testimonial evidence from one spouse for use in the prosecution of the other spouse. Of course, Richard did not tell Tish everything.

"Sweet dreams, dear." Richard looked at her bottom in the mirrors. As if Tish had eyes in the back of her head, she abruptly pulled up the sheet. Richard yawned again. She was a pretty blonde thing.

Richard turned off the brass lamp. The soft patter of the rain on the windowpanes was the last thing Richard heard before he fell asleep.

* * *

When Jeff Burke got back into his office in Baltimore after an uneventful drive from Washington, he was greeted with some bad news. One of his cases was settled in court in favor of the taxpayer.

The story had begun about two years ago. One of his informers had provided Jeff with a short list of some high-priced prostitutes. One name was a real pro.

Jeff obtained a search warrant and while searching her luxurious apartment found a small piece of gray luggage, which was completely filled with stacks of money. The sight of all that money had made the back of his neck tingle and a chill go down his spine. When counted, the money totaled $50,055. Jeff also found her "John book."

When confronted, she shrugged her shoulders and indicated that the money was gifts from several of her gentlemen friends. Gifts, of course, are not taxable. At this point Jeff had Collections slap a jeopardy assessment on her for the entire amount and took her money.

A jeopardy assessment is used when the tax is already due and payable but the activities of the taxpayer jeopardize its collection. This procedure is used where the IRS believes that the taxpayer may remove or transfer the property, the taxpayer may quickly depart from the United States, the taxpayer may conceal herself or her property, or do other acts which might frustrate collection of the tax liability. The procedure is often applied to suspected criminal offenders involved in gambling, narcotics, or other illegal activities. Property may be seized by the IRS pending determination of the issue in the court.

Jeff was able to calculate her income with a method upheld by the court in a famous IRS case where two towels per John was used to estimate the income of a brothel. He obtained laundry lists from her laundry. She had made the mistake of renting her sheets and changing her sheets after each customer.

Her "John book" indicated a rate of $400 per date. She had a first-class operation! The laundry lists indicated that she had two dates per day at $400 per date, three weeks per month, twelve months per year—less, of course, appropriate expenses for her sheets. The IRS computer showed that she had not filed tax returns for the previous four years.

Jeff thought he had her. But she hired a smart tax lawyer. She voluntarily filed tax returns for the four years involved. On the fourth she reported gross income of $51,000. Although there was a substantial tax due on this amount, she claimed that she had already *paid* $50,055. She asked for *a refund of* $44,000. Obviously, the IRS refused to give her the refund.

She went to court. The issue before the court was whether a refund was due and not the propriety of her tax returns. The judge accepted her tax returns at face value and ordered the IRS to refund her money *with interest.*

Jeff was depressed. He had worked on this case for about two years. There was consolation; the length of a usual fraud case could be more than two years.

Jeff sighed deeply and turned his attention to the Onner problem. His returns appeared to be okay. Jeff chuckled when he saw that three years before Onner had claimed a dependency exemption for an unrelated woman with whom he lived that year. Onner also had used the special head of household rate in computing his income tax. An individual who is a member of a taxpayer's household for the *entire* year does not have to be related to the taxpayer in order for the taxpayer to claim the individual as a personal exemption.

But Jeff recalled that there had been a court decision several years ago, which disallowed the dependency exemption and head of household rates for the breadwinner of an unmarried couple. The court held that cohabitation was illegal under local law. The decision had lacked any evidence as to habitual sexual intercourse. In other words, the taxpayers had not taken any avowals of celibacy. Jeff wondered if Onner and his girlfriend had taken such an avowal, or whether the act of living with his claimed dependent violated West Virginia law.

The telephone on his desk buzzed softly. The switchboard operator indicated that Yvonne Talbert was on the other end. "Hello, Yvonne."

"Hi, Jeff. Thought I would remind you of my conference with Carl Strovee on Wednesday at 3:00 p.m. Could you be here at 2:00 p.m. to go over the details? I believe we have a fraud case, but my blasted supervisor is putting pressure on me to close the case."

"Is he the ESP character who makes all those weird predictions?" Jeff asked.

"Yes. I hope he can predict how many years he will get when we put the noose around his neck. After I interview Strovee, I would like to talk to you. See you on Wednesday."

"Good-bye."

Jeff, of course, knew what Yvonne meant by "pressure from her supervisor." Yvonne was a Revenue Agent, and she worked under unofficial quotas with respect to the number of cases closed and the amount of tax revenues she obtains. Most taxpayers were unaware of the fact that an IRS agent wants a short audit, while collecting as much revenue as possible.

Yvonne had once told Jeff that her supervisor kept a computer record of the number of closed cases and the new revenue collected by each of his agents. Thus, each agent had to produce.

In public, the IRS always denied that there were quotas. While the Internal Revenue Service Restructuring and Reform Act of 1998 ended the formal evaluation of agent performance based upon the amount of revenue collected, it was still an informal yardstick of success. They still existed unofficially in some offices. Promotions were slow for those agents who fell below the norm. Obviously, a Revenue Agent had to find at least enough "juice" to cover his or her salary. In recent years, no-change audits have moved from less than 20 percent to above 25 percent of all tax audits.

By the time Jeff was finished with his paperwork it was 6:30 p.m. He drove over to Calvert Street to Flesher Printing Company. A gloomy sky hung over the skyline of Baltimore. Mr. Flesher was a "numbered" or "jacketed" case. After the department had decided to follow through with a fraud case, it was given a number. Each Special Agent also had six or seven non-numbered cases. These latter cases had not reached the stage that fraud or a criminal activity was a certainty.

Flesher Printing Company was involved with the football cards racket. The print shop had been under surveillance by Jeff for three weeks. Maybe tonight Jeff would be lucky.

Jeff thought the print shop did the printing of the tickets for the numbers racket in Baltimore. A printer always prints several practice runs before beginning a printing job. Jeff had been checking the garbage dumpster in the back of the shop for three weeks. An agent's life is not always pleasant, Jeff was thinking, as he rummaged through the garbage. Tonight Jeff found a handful of spaghetti and a brochure for a forensic accounting seminar. Certainly not enough for a fraud conviction!

There was an important difference between a civil conviction and a criminal conviction. In a civil tax prosecution where the IRS has assessed a deficiency, the taxpayer generally has the burden of proof. The taxpayer must prove that he owes no deficiency. In other words, the taxpayer is presumed to be guilty until he proves himself innocent since the taxpayer's filed tax return is a self-declaration of income, expenses, and deductions.

But the burden of proof is upon the IRS in a *criminal* or fraud prosecution. The IRS must prove that the taxpayer willfully intended to defraud. Intent is hard to prove. Or the IRS must prove the criminal activities. Here, the taxpayer is presumed to be innocent until the IRS proves him guilty beyond a reasonable doubt.

Jeff was trying to obtain evidence for a criminal prosecution. The Department of Justice handles criminal tax litigation.

Intent is extremely difficult to prove. You have to get inside the person's mind. That's why many Special Agents feel that they have higher status than anyone else in law enforcement.

Consider the function of an FBI agent. He only has to prove that a car was stolen in one state and found in another state. The FBI agent does not have to prove that the person willfully intended to cross the state line.

Jeff recalled a favorite joke of Special Agents. Compared to a Special Agent, an FBI agent couldn't track an elephant with a nose-bleed over fresh snow. In the past there has been competition and friction between the IRS and the FBI. Often the IRS would prepare income tax cases against underworld figures, murderers, political bosses, and other criminals who were otherwise untouchable by the FBI. The FBI would get the credit and publicity, and the IRS was left with only resentment.

For example, Nick "Greasy Thumb" Guzik, treasurer of the Al Capone gang, was one of the many top gangsters caught by Special Agents. "Greasy Thumb" got his nickname from the green stain on his hands from counting cash. Handwriting experts convinced a bank cashier to "spill his guts" about "Greasy Thumb," and he was indicted, convicted, and sent to prison for five years.

On the way home Jeff fortified himself with a sausage pizza at the Pizza Hut. That night while watching David Letterman, Jeff fell asleep sitting on his ice pack. He dreamed about sliding down the snowy ski slopes in Snowmass, Colorado. At the end of Fanny Hill he fell into the icy-cold Frying Pan River. He had skied at both Aspen, the Victorian town, and Snowmass several years earlier. He also had gone fly fishing in the river near Basalt. When he awoke the next morning he was shivering.

Chapter 4

People who squawk about their income taxes may be divided into two classes. They are: men and women.

—Anonymous

Jeff was up early and had gulped down only one cup of hot green
tea for breakfast. Since 8:00 a.m. he had been sitting in his car
watching the entrance to a modest brownstone on St. Paul Street.

It was now 9:10 a.m., and he was bored. Rob Fowler was under
surveillance. He was a suspected "runner" for the football-betting
racket in Baltimore. A runner is the person who goes around collecting the bets placed during the day.

At 9:11 Rob emerged from his house with his companion. She
was both old and fat. Rob was a tall, lanky, young black man with
a short hairdo with a part carved into the right side. His trademark
must be a silk shirt this morning.

Twice a week Jeff had to follow Rob. Other agents followed Rob
on the other weekdays. There was a problem. For two weeks no
one had been able to follow Rob because he was a "crazy" driver.

Rob and his "lady" got into a light tan 2007 Ford. All the runners drove this same type and color of car. This caused havoc with
surveillance operations.

The tan Ford took the same route as the previous mornings.
Rob dropped off his "lady" at a plumbing outlet. Out to the Beltway the Ford moved. Jeff had to "run" two stoplights along the way
to keep up with the tan car.

The traffic was still heavy on the Beltway. Jeff mumbled, "I'll get
you today." The target car stayed in the right lane for about four
miles. Up ahead was a Budweiser beer truck going about fifty miles

an hour. This truck caused Jeff to get too close to Rob. Traffic was
bunched up. All of a sudden Rob swerved left across two lanes. His
car almost took off a bumper on the car next to him.

Jeff could do nothing. There was no way he could get across to
the far-left lane because he was hemmed in. Rob sped away. Rob
had won again.

Jeff cursed. In two days, he reminded himself, he would have a
search warrant to search Rob's house.

Once Jeff was satisfied that he had really lost Rob, he shrugged
and turned around and headed for Washington. As he had promised, he would check on Richard Onner.

After bypassing Washington, Jeff listened to the chatter on a talk
radio show as he passed through Germantown, Brunswick, and
Sandy Hook, Maryland.

When he got to Sheperdstown, West Virginia, he knew he was
close to Martinsburg. He had not yet decided what to do. Maybe
he would go to Antietam National Battlefield and finesse Onner. A
pothole in the road and the resulting pain in his groin reminded Jeff
that he did not wish to walk around on a hilly battlefield.

Jeff followed the signs to Martinsburg. No one had yet prepared
a bank deposit analysis on Onner. Jeff felt that Onner was not dumb
enough to deposit any unreported income in a bank. But he would
canvass the banks anyway.

Jeff stopped at a telephone booth near a Best Western Motel and
copied down the names and addresses of the banks in Martinsburg
and Onner's telephone number.

At each bank Jeff talked to the managers and showed them his
Special Agent badge. Most of them gulped, then smiled and said,
"Yes, sir," once he showed them his summons.

The life of a Special Agent can be dull. Some of the most important evidence that an agent can obtain during an investigation
will be found in banks and other financial institutions. Jeff was
thankful for his accounting background.

Agents must examine bank records such as canceled checks and
bank statements. Extremely important are the teller's daily record

sheets, which are maintained by the bank but are not made available to the taxpayer. Teller's cash receipts will disclose transactions where the taxpayer cashed checks to obtain money for a deposit or for himself. Such an activity is contrary to normal business practice and may indicate that the checks were not reported as income.

There are two types of bank canvassing. Jeff could either write the bank or make a personal visit to the bank. Under either method, a summons letter should be prepared and presented to the bank official. Jeff had not prepared the necessary letters, but the bank officials did not ask for anything.

A bank should ask for a service of a summons before permitting an examination of a taxpayer's accounts. He knew that the Fourth and Fifth Amendments do not shield information voluntarily given by the taxpayer-depositor to his bank. Also, a taxpayer is entitled to advance notice of the IRS's intention to examine the bank records within 3 days, but no later than 23 days. A taxpayer may intervene and try to quash the production of records. Eventually the court has to decide.

Sometimes Jeff had to go through the bank records himself. That was a time-consuming, boring task. Often, investigative aides were used to go through tedious book records. When many banks' computer records were involved, Jeff often photographed the records. The managers of both banks seemed to be willing to prepare the appropriate schedules. They were willing to reproduce Onner's checks from their records. Jeff didn't complain.

Onner had a checking account at one bank and a savings account at another bank. Jeff asked the managers to prepare a schedule of Onner's transactions for the past three years. He left his business card, asking them to send the appropriate schedules to his Baltimore office.

At both banks Onner had a safe deposit box. Jeff asked for copies of the safe deposit boxes' access records, which show dates and times of entries along with the signature of the person entering the box. These dates and frequency of entries may be important, for they may coincide with the dates of deposits to or withdrawals from other accounts.

For many years the IRS could not enter a safe deposit box without getting the box holder's permission. An agent would have to contact the box holder and get his consent to inventory the contents of the box in the presence of the box holder. If the taxpayer objected, the agent could only write up a memorandum of the refusal.

But individual privacy bit the dust in 1977, in the Citibank case. The U.S. Court of Appeals in New York held that the IRS had the legal right to break open a taxpayer's safe deposit box to search for valuables *without giving the box holder the right to object.* Jeff wondered what was in the safe deposit boxes.

Part 4 of Form 668-B must be given to the bank to search a safe deposit box. Banks are excellent sources of leads for Special Agents. Leads are often found in the Currency Transaction Reports made by banks to their Federal Reserve Bank for cash transactions of $10,000 or above. These CTR's may disclose large cash deposits and withdrawals. Banks get about 100,000 summons a year to provide customer records to the IRS.

Treasury Regulations prescribe certain bank record keeping and reporting requirements. Regulations are four volumes of administrative interpretations prepared by the Treasury Department that explain the legislative Internal Revenue Code. Customers' identities must be maintained and checks must be microfilmed. Domestic cash transactions and other monetary instruments such as money orders exceeding $3,000 in or out of the U.S. must be documented by financial institutions.

The then Governor of New York Eliot Spitzer was caught in a prostitution scandal when the North Fork Bank reported his suspicious actions to the IRS. Spitzer, aka George Fox, broke up cash transactions into small slices to get under the $10,000 threshold in order to transfer funds to a prostitution business. Of course, he later had a television show on CNN. Go figure.

Personal checks are excluded. Pete Rose received $129,000 from selling the baseball bat that he used to break Ty Cobb's record for most hits. Pete Rose had the buyer give him separate checks so that no single one was more than $10,000. Rose must have been confused about the requirement that banks report *cash* transactions. Obviously there is a difference between cash and checks.

Rose was fined $50,000 and received five months in jail for failure to report $345,967 of memorabilia income. Duke Snider and Willie McCovey pleaded guilty in July 1995 for tax evasion charges for memorabilia income.

In one situation Jeff became interested in a report of two deposits by a Report of Currency Transactions furnished by a Federal Reserve Bank. There were two bank deposits of $20,000 each in old, crumpled, tissue paper-thin $100 bills. The condition of the money suggested that it had been stored in an unusual place for a considerable period of time. Jeff caused a summons to be issued directing the bank to identify the owner or owners of the deposited money. Here the bank refused to provide the identity of the owner. In court the bank won. The Court said that a summons seeking the identity of a taxpayer, rather than details concerning an already identified taxpayer, was generally not enforceable under the Internal Revenue Code. The IRS does not always win.

But the IRS won in another situation. Another agent was investigating the possible income tax violation of an individual who had deposited $45,000 in deteriorated $100 bills into a Kentucky bank. The IRS issued a summons requiring the bank to provide the identity of the depositor. The bank refused to comply, but eventually the Supreme Court upheld the summons. The IRS got their taxpayer.

After eating a hamburger and drinking a milkshake at a Burger King, Jeff drove to Onner's townhouse. He observed the townhouse for about thirty minutes. He then telephoned Onner's number, but no one answered. He then walked through the private courtyard to Onner's door and rang the doorbell twice. He left. Jeff believed in checking out the lifestyles of taxpayers. Behavioral aspects of a person were important to him. A great deal can be learned by listening, especially around the copy machine and break room.

Jeff watched the door for fifteen minutes more. He then returned and rang the doorbell again. When no one answered, he quickly picked the lock and entered through an atrium filled with plants. He pulled on some thin rubber gloves.

Jeff normally did not break and enter without a warrant. Anything he found would not be admissible in court. Besides, if discovered, he could be in trouble. But maybe he could locate some leads as to how Onner was getting his money.

As he entered the living room of the townhouse he noticed the natural wood beams on the ceiling. The door casing and woodwork were of natural wood also. The townhouse was furnished quite nicely. Several expensive-looking paintings were on the wall. There was an antique corn sheller on an old Singer sewing machine. On a coffee table were a *U.S. News & World Report*, a *Coin World* newspaper, a *Consumer Reports*, a *Hang Gliding*, and a *Photography*. On the wall was an enlarged photograph of someone hang gliding.

In a bookcase Jeff noticed the book *How to Do Business Tax-Free: A Guide to Tax Havens*. Jeff rummaged through the letters and papers on a small desk and found the typical bills, a notice of the forthcoming meeting of the Martinsburg Coin Club, and a copy of a newsletter entitled "How to Cheat and Defraud the IRS," by I. M. Clever.

Jeff glanced at the first tax technique discussed in the newsletter. It dealt with silver coins. The author suggested that retailers might wish to sell their merchandise for dimes, quarters and half-dollars minted before 1965 with a 90% silver content. Such coins sell for almost 20 times their face value.

The article indicated that an Oklahoma Volkswagen dealer was offering the best deal anywhere featuring the popular new Jetta with a price tag of only $3,720—if paid for with these silver coins.

The car dealer would pay his wholesaler with fiat paper money for his car inventory. The dealer could avoid income taxes because his income is measured in silver coins at face value while his expenses are measured in fiat paper money. Jeff jumped when Onner's phone began to ring.

Jeff picked up a small note pad and wrote down the name of the newsletter, the author, and mailing address. He could probably collect some "juice" if he could somehow get a list of the subscribers to this trash. He carefully replaced the note pad in its proper location.

As he put the newsletter back on the table he noticed an ad in the "classified" section:

> Sue IRS Agents or other governmental officials who violate your Civil Rights. To file a $150 suit without a lawyer send $80 to TPE, P.O. Box 2815, Turkey, N.C., 28393 for full information about affidavits, case law, etc.

Jeff felt a chill on his skin as he remembered that he had illegally broken into Onner's apartment. The phone stopped ringing, and Jeff moved into another room.

Jeff was impressed when he walked into one of the two bedrooms. There was an unmade king-size waterbed with mirrors on the ceiling and a bearskin rug on the floor. In the mirrors Jeff saw how funny he walked trying to avoid pain from his injury. He also made a mental note to lose a couple of pounds.

Jeff froze in his tracks when he heard a key enter a door lock. Luckily, it was the next door neighbor entering his townhouse.

Jeff got a light blue Kleenex from the bathroom and quickly moved to the front door. He took off his gloves and used the Kleenex to open the door. Quickly and carefully he went outside, pulling the door closed and wiping off the doorknob and doorbell. A car drove into the parking lot as Jeff made his way towards his Chevrolet. Off he went with a jump-start and a sigh of relief, thinking he would try to find a motel with an indoor swimming pool. Not likely in this town. "What do I want to eat tonight? Maybe I'll shoot some pool."

* * *

Richard Onner was flying like a bird. He was strapped in a harness fastened to a dacron sail. Richard had worked two Saturdays and today was his day off. He was defying gravity, flying without an airplane. He saw high, fast moving white clouds above his head.

Soaring like a bird, looking around at the earth, a thrill of excitement traveled through his body. Richard had been hang gliding since he was 15.

His rig of dacron was fitted with an aluminum and stainless steel frame, which was thirty feet wide. His glider contained two hundred square feet of sail in its fifty pounds. A bird flew by as Richard made a right turn.

The chances of a hang gliding participant being injured are greater than those for most other sports participants. For hang gliding, the chance of death is 1 out of 116,000 versus bungee jumping of 1 out of 500,000. Accidents are more common among experienced hang-gliders who fly higher, go farther, and take greater risks than novices.

Richard's father had been a glider. He was killed when a gust of wind blew him into a cliff in the hilly Vermont area. Most deaths and injuries were caused by pilot carelessness, flights during gusty winds, lack of preparation for landings, and tricky air turbulence.

Richard was extremely careful today. But he was unaware of the intruder who had entered, searched, and left his townhouse.

* * *

Jimmy Callaway was the Commissioner of the Internal Revenue Service, which had a $12.6 billion annual budget. As the Commissioner, he reported to the Secretary of the Treasury. He was the boss of 106,000 employees handling billions of documents, working in seven regional offices, 33 district offices, and 8 service centers. In a recent year, the IRS processed more than 236 million tax returns and collected more than $2.3 trillion in revenue. He was responsible for the administration of all tax laws. Yet the IRS fails to collect more than $300 billion of taxes a year; as the IRS staff has declined the tax returns have increased. The number of IRS agents and criminal investigators fell about 30 percent from 1996 to 2002. As the fear of an audit declines, the more tax cheating will occur. The personnel number has recently increased, especially with Obamacare.

The IRS is only one of ten sections within the Treasury Department. The IRS manual indicates the following mission of the IRS:

> Provide America's taxpayers top quality service by helping them understand and meet their tax responsibilities and enforce the tax law with integrity and fairness to all.

The Commissioner of the IRS is a political appointee. Jimmy was the token Southerner in the current administration. He was a tall, boyish-looking man. His black hair was slightly graying at the temples. A carbon copy of the perennial politician.

Callaway was a product of the "yellow-dog" era in North Carolina politics. The term "yellow-dog" was used to describe the situation in the South whereby Southerners would vote Democratic no matter who ran on the ticket. It was said that people would pull the Democrat lever even if a yellow dog were the Democratic candidate. There still are a lot of these yellow-dog Democrats in states like Louisiana.

Callaway was born in Lizard Lick, North Carolina. A small community in Wake County, it was named by a passing observer who saw many lizards sunning and licking themselves on a rail fence.

Being from a safe district, he became a powerful senator in the North Carolina legislature. A shirtsleeves campaigner, he was as comfortable making the rounds of the political barrooms as he was in the corporate boardrooms. He dominated the Senate where few Republicans were allowed to enter. He simply trampled down any opposition. Today Republicans control the N.C. Senate.

Although a Democrat, he was relatively conservative. Callaway was a former cotton baron, a banker, and a businessman. He was an early supporter of Bill Clinton and was rewarded with a middle-level position in the Clinton administration. He hung on in Washington after Clinton. He was later appointed Commissioner of the Internal Revenue Service by President Keeney. Callaway had the one requirement for the position: he was a lawyer. There had been few non-lawyers to hold this position.

Callaway briefly skimmed the letter in front of him. He had an important meeting with Congressman Blackman.

Personal

Honorable Jimmy Callaway
Commissioner of Internal Revenue Service
1111 Constitution Avenue
Washington, D.C. 20220

Dear Commissioner Callaway:

Per IRS Directive #2031, I am reporting that Richard Onner, a computer employee with the IRS in Martinsburg, WV, is under surveillance for possible income tax evasion. A net worth analysis indicates about $33,000 of unreported income per year.
I have asked Special Agent Jeff Burke (Baltimore) to help with this investigation.

Sincerely,

Nick Anderson
Special Agent, TIGTA

NA:ddt
cc: Jeff Burke

Commissioner Callaway left immediately for his meeting with Congressman Blackman. The Congressman was still a powerful legislator. Congressman Blackman was the Chairman of the important House Ways and Means Committee. This committee was the beginning of all tax laws. Even the President of the United States had to introduce tax laws through this committee. This committee controlled the inflow of all Federal revenues.

Although extremely powerful, the Chairman of the Ways and Means Committee had even more power until the late 1970s. This was the time when Fanny Foxe took her infamous early morning swim in the Tidal Basin while with Wilbur Mills. This event destroyed the effectiveness of the then Congressman Wilbur Mills, who was Chairman of Ways and Means.

Congress stripped some of the power away from the Chairman of this Committee. The succeeding Chairmen, Al Ullman, Dan Rostenkowski, and Blackman, never became quite the kingpin ex-Representative Wilbur Mills had been before the Fanny Foxe incident. Poor Rostenkowski even went to jail. Of course, Charlie Rangel was removed from the chairmanship position in 2010 for not paying his taxes.

What was the news report that he had heard last week? Some ex-politicians had indicated that they had created a Politicians' Anonymous. Each time an ex-politician felt the urge to run for public office, he could dial a number and then P.A. would send over Fanny Foxe, and they could jump into the Tidal Basin together.

His black limousine was waiting for him when he got downstairs. His personal chauffeur drove him to "the Hill." Yes, the "perks" had come back after Reagan, Bush, Clinton, and Bush. They skyrocketed when Obama took charge.

Chapter 5

I don't suppose we will ever get to the point where people are pleased to pay taxes.

—Lyndon B. Johnson

Wednesday morning had been nonproductive for Jeff. He had driven over to see the "Martinsburg Computer Monster." The clean, clinical-looking building with the multilevel floors impressed Jeff. There were false floors under which there was vacant space filled with miles of electrical cords and other necessary equipment needed by the computers. This hidden space was kept at a cold 60 degrees temperature. The temperature in the rooms was kept at a constant 76 degrees with 55% humidity.

Jeff talked to a friend and saw the organization and operation of the computer center. He had seen Richard Onner from afar, but he had not talked to him. He had not asked anyone about him.

He made the uneventful drive back to Baltimore in time to meet Yvonne Talbert at 2:00 p.m. Yvonne had a round fat face and had a few gray hairs in her wavy brown hair. She was forty-fiveish.

"Hello, Yvonne," Jeff said as he interrupted Yvonne in deep thought. "What do you have for me today?"

Yvonne shifted in her chair and said enthusiastically: "Glad you came, Jeff. This is one you'll like. I believe I have it sewn up. Do you want a cold drink?" pointing to a small refrigerator in the corner.

"Nope. Trying to keep my weight down. Haven't had any decent exercise in about a week. You heard about my accident, didn't you?"

"Jeez, sounded bad. Getting any better?"

"Guess so," responded Jeff.

45

"Carl Strovee will be here at 3:00 p.m. I believe his representative is Henry Silverman. He is not a CPA. Silverman is a con artist. He's a cocky punk." Yvonne was noted for her bluntness.

Yvonne took a drink from a can of Diet Coke and continued. "I audited Strovee's tax return last year. Couldn't find a dime. But I just knew he was ripping us off."

"I canvassed the banks here in Baltimore, but my bank deposit analysis of him did not show anything unusual. Then I read some biographical advertisement about him. He is from Valentine, Nebraska. I asked our Omaha office to check the banks in Valentine.

"Bingo! His retired mother has a bank account in Valentine, and he has been depositing money into her account. Using the bank deposit method, I added together all of his bank deposits, and deducted the gross income on his tax return. There was a big difference. In the past three years he has been hiding about 30% of his gross income."

Yvonne paused, took a measured drink from her Diet Coke, and then continued. "My supervisor is trying to get me to assess the tax with civil penalties and close the case. I wish you would make a preliminary examination. Until the criminal aspects are settled, will you be responsible for the direction taken by the investigation? I'm willing to keep it open. I believe we can nail him."

"Okay, but let's see what happens at the conference at three o'clock. I'll wait around until you finish."

The Strovee case was following the typical scenario of a fraud investigation. A taxpayer submits his tax return to the IRS, and it goes through the IRS computer. For one reason or another, the tax return is selected for audit. The higher the taxable income, the greater chance of an audit. Or perhaps the return is selected at random. Or the IRS might decide to concentrate on taxpayers in a particular profession.

For whatever reason, the audit procedure starts when a taxpayer gets a letter from the IRS informing him that his return is to be examined and specifying whether the examination is an office or field audit. There are basically two types of office audits — a correspondence audit and an office interview audit. A correspondence audit is carried on by mail between the taxpayer and an office auditor. It is most often limited to the verification of minor items; whereas, in an office interview audit the taxpayer is asked to bring certain supporting records to an IRS office where he or she is interviewed by an Office Auditor. A field audit is used for business returns and complex individual returns. Here the Revenue Agent goes to the business premises to conduct the audit.

A Revenue Agent had suspected Carl Strovee of tax fraud. Yvonne Talbert had asked an Intelligence Officer in Omaha to check for possible bank accounts in Valentine. The Omaha office had found his mother's bank account.

With some incriminating evidence in hand, Yvonne still needed *someone* from the Intelligence Division to investigate the case. Jeff was being asked to help with the investigation. He would not attend the examination, however.

A revenue agent who is conducting a civil examination is not required to advise the taxpayer of his or her constitutional rights or to advise a taxpayer that a routine civil audit may result in criminal proceedings. But a Special Agent must give such warning when there is a criminal investigation.

Henry Silverman had encouraged Carl Strovee not to attend the conference at three o'clock. From experience Henry knew that individuals sometimes become indignant and belligerent when their integrity and honesty are being questioned. Even worse, taxpayers sometimes have a severe attack of foot-in-mouth disease and provide too much information to the agents. Talking too much raises areas of examination that the agent was not even considering.

Henry knew that with an agent, you had to be friendly and answer the exact question asked. There was no reason to provide extra information, which might complicate what might otherwise be a simple problem. Henry had never dealt with Yvonne Talbert. But he had heard that she was a "bird dog."

Carl had not heeded Henry's advice. He was going to attend the conference. Carl and Henry arrived at the same time, and they walked together to Room 2001. Carl was very skinny, with bleached hair, wearing a diamond earring in his left ear.

Yvonne was already in the room when Carl and Henry arrived. Yvonne walked over and closed the door, which bore a bright blue "Do Not Disturb" sign.

Yvonne introduced herself to Henry and Carl. Yvonne immediately asked for a Form 2848. Henry handed Yvonne a copy of the "Power of Attorney," signed by Carl, giving Henry the right to represent his client.

Yvonne had a Form 4700 Supplement in front of her, which is often used by office auditors. This form has many questions to ask the taxpayer, with a spot check "yes" or "no" for each response from the taxpayer. Yvonne needed to go down this standardized list to establish that Carl did not have a cash hoard or income from nontaxable sources.

After Carl confirmed that he had no cash hoard, Yvonne spoke to Henry in a soft voice. "Could we see the back-up for the Section 1244 stock?" Henry handed Yvonne the minutes page. Yvonne presented Henry a receipt for the sheet. "We wish to keep the minutes until next Wednesday."

"Is that necessary?" responded Henry in an angry tone.

"Yes, Mr. Silverman. You are aware that the election for Section 1244 stock should occur at the creation of the corporation."

"True, but the minutes were drafted in the first year," shot back Henry, as the pitch of his voice rose.

"Mr. Silverman, your client has failed to pay $67,554 of taxes, over the past three years, including interest and penalties," Yvonne said softly. A fleeting smile came and left Yvonne's face.

Carl Strovee shouted, "What?" His eyes were blinking wildly.

Yvonne knew that the blinking indicated the thinking and feeling process. A high rate of blinking is associated with thoughts that are disturbing or frustrating. Carl was clearly disturbed.

The meeting was not following the normal pattern. Agents are instructed to establish a rapport with the taxpayer and his representative in a friendly, affable manner to establish the confidence of the taxpayer. They should keep the conversation informal and easy. The objective of such a tactic is to elicit information about the taxpayer's family, gambling, vacations, acquisition of major assets, hobbies, and other expenditures to determine whether the taxpayer is living beyond his reported income.

A friendly approach may encourage the taxpayer and/or representative to answer more honestly since he does not know why the questions are being asked. In theory, the friendly approach gives the taxpayer a false sense of security, and the agent may be able to get information that would not otherwise be revealed. Form 4822 is used by an agent to record the information gathered during the interview.

Yvonne did not respond to Carl's outburst. Agents are trained to ignore taxpayer anger and grumbling and remain polite.

For a moment he was uncomfortable, but Henry calmly responded, "I have prepared Mr. Strovee's tax returns for the past five years. You must be mistaken. Carl could not owe that much money. How did you come up with such a figure?"

With a smile of triumph on her face Yvonne responded, "Our bank deposits analysis indicated that Mr. Strover has not been reporting about 30% of his income per year." Yvonne withdrew the Strovee calculations and bank documents from a manila folder on the conference table.

In a combative voice, Henry said, "It's Mr. Strovee, not Strover!" At the same time he looked questioningly toward Carl Strovee. Henry had clearly told Carl not to deposit the unreported receipts into his bank account.

In a low voice Carl replied, "I do not believe I owe such a deficiency. My bank records will verify that I have reported all of my income."

Trying to hold back her smile, Yvonne asked, "But what about your mother's bank accounts in Valentine?" Yvonne held up the confirmation letter from the Valentine bank. For a few seconds the only sound in the room was from Yvonne's small fan.

There was a sinking feeling in the bottom of Carl's stomach. Those IRS gumshoes had found his secret Valentine account.

From the look on Carl's face, Henry guessed what Carl had been doing. He immediately stood up. "Carl, it is time for us to leave. We need a lawyer," he said acidly.

Carl slowly got up. His eyes were no longer blinking. His thoughts were turned inward. Why had he done such a stupid thing—putting the deposits in the Valentine account?

Yvonne interrupted Carl's thoughts. "I want you to prepare me a statement of net worth for the past five years. Could you get this information to me by next Wednesday?"

Carl nodded.

But Yvonne had still another surprise for Mr. Silverman. Yvonne handed Henry an official piece of paper. It was an IRS summons signed by Jeff Burke.

The summons required Henry Silverman to appear the next Wednesday at the same time and place and to produce his working papers and other records relating to Carl Strovee and to give oral testimony. "Mr. Silverman, would you sign this Certificate of Service of Summons? It merely means that you have received the Summons," Yvonne explained. Henry signed the certificate.

Suddenly Henry Silverman had a headache. He remembered that he had in his possession a copy of the true income of Carl. Jeez, I should have given those records to Carl before today's meeting. I need to work under an attorney's umbrella of privilege, using a "three corner agreement."

The Fifth Amendment to the Constitution provides that "No person ... shall be compelled to be a witness against himself." This privilege includes the right to refuse to surrender one's *personal* records which one feels will tend to incriminate him. But this Fifth Amendment privilege does *not* extend to records of an accountant, which might incriminate another taxpayer.

Henry knew that although this summons was issued by an administrative agency, the summons is similar to the investigative-type of grand jury subpoena. Thus, if Henry did not honor the summons, the court could arrest and punish him with a jail sentence or a fine for contempt.

Both Henry and Carl left immediately. Outside Henry tried to explain to Carl that if a taxpayer disagrees with the initial audit by a Revenue Agent, he may protest any deficiency with an Appeals Officer. "Discussions with the Appeals Officer can solve many conflicts. Look, dealings with the IRS are a 'cat-and-mouse' game, with compromises possible at all levels within the IRS and even on the court house steps.

"Where no solution is agreed upon with the IRS, a taxpayer has three appeal choices when a 'notice of deficiency' or '90-day letter' is issued. You can pay the deficiency and after denial of claim for refund, file an action in the District Court, where a jury trial is possible, or in the Court of Federal Claims, which is in Washington, D.C. Likewise, you can refuse to pay the tax and file a petition with the Tax Court—the poor person's court. The Small Cases Division of the Tax Court is available for a deficiency less than $50,000."

Carl broke in, saying, "I should have listened to one of my friends' advice."

"What's that?"

"He said that I should have my tax return prepared by a CPA. The chances of an audit are much higher if a return is personally prepared or is prepared by a non-professional tax preparer."

"I'm a professional!" shot back Henry.

"But you're not a CPA."

Henry just shook his head and replied coldly, "Keep your mouth shut and find a good lawyer." Henry knew that Carl's financial affairs were in the IRS's vise, with the handle slowly being turned. However, Carl was not the only famous person to have trouble with the IRS.

In fact, Carl was in "good" company. Al Capone could only be sent to jail for income tax evasion. Vice-President Spiro Agnew pleaded *nolo contendere* to income tax evasion. Representative Adam Clayton Powell was indicted for income tax evasion. Bobby Parker, a protege of Lyndon Johnson, was convicted for evading taxes. And Joe Louis, the famous "Brown Bomber," had problems with the IRS throughout his fighting career. Remember Jerry Lee Lewis' tax problems? In 1990, the IRS seized Willie Nelson's property in six states to satisfy $6.5 million in tax claims.

Even after Jimmy Hoffa disappeared, he was not forgotten by the IRS. The IRS claimed he owed $40,000 of back taxes, and they went after his widow.

After Duke Ellington died in 1974, the IRS claimed that his estate owed $1.4 million for taxes and penalties for 1967–1973. The IRS disallowed big deductions for travel, clothing, and other business expenses. Also, the IRS alleged that the musician did not report certain income from television appearances.

Many people do not realize it, but even illegal income is taxable. A "smart" crook should report illegal income, maybe under the category of miscellaneous income.

The IRS never forgets. For example, a skyjacker vanished somewhere between Seattle and Reno in 1971. By 1976, Dan Cooper, the skyjacker, owed the IRS $218,635 in taxes on the money he extorted. The IRS calculated his tax with a substitute for a return, assuming he was alive, single, and never filed a return for the illegal money. He owed $123,090 plus a 50% civil fraud penalty because he intended to cheat the government out of their share of the extortion money. Interest at 7% a year is $34,000, for a total tax burden of $218,635 from the illegal income.

After her interview Yvonne explained to Jeff what had transpired.

Jeff was in a good mood when he got back to his office and sat down at his desk. In the center of his desk was a plain envelope addressed "To Super Jock." Jeff removed a card from the envelope. On the front was

This card was designed for a typical, well-adjusted Normal Human Being.

Inside in black letters was

But we bought it for you anyway! Get Well.

Jeff chuckled as he read the comments written by members of his softball team:

Get Well Soon! *TKM*	You're not normal. *Daniel*	I think it may help! *Bud*
Who needs sex? *Hank*	Watch out for the rebound. *Joe*	Join a Glee Club. *Harold*
Why the shorter steps? *Steve*	Better visit the sporting goods store. *Mike*	Next time move faster. *Caleb*

The team didn't win many softball games, but they had a good sense of humor. Jeff wondered if they had won Monday night. Jeff wrote on his "to do" list to go by the sporting goods store and purchase a "steel jock."

On the way home Jeff was again disappointed. His search of the Flesher garbage dumpster resulted in only one broken mouse trap and a torn romance novel—*See Mary Run.*

Chapter 6

In levying taxes and in shearing sheep, it is well to stop when you get down to skin.

—Austin O' Malley

Wednesday morning at 8:00 Jeff was again watching the brownstone house. He and another agent were waiting for Rob Fowler to emerge and drive off in his tan Ford.

Hank Brown, his companion, was wearily sipping coffee. He was trying to stay awake for what would be the ensuing chase through Baltimore. Hank's grim humor and his slightly balding head made him a perfect IRS sleuth. Hank was in his early thirties, and he had been with the IRS for ten years. He liked to carry his .357 Colt Python. Hank was divorced with one child who lived with his ex-wife in Selma, Alabama. Hank liked to drink beer at a joint near the IRS office, which reminded him of his hometown, Selma.

Hank played first base on Jeff's softball team. He hit a lot of home runs, but he was slow and had a short temper. He constantly argued with the umpires.

In the game in which Jeff was hurt, Hank had been thrown out of the ball game in the second inning. A batter had hit a ground ball to the third baseman. The throw to Hank at first base had pulled him toward home plate. The running batter had brushed Hank's left leg as he passed in the baseline.

Hank got angry. He turned around and threw the softball at the runner. The softball hit the runner in the small of his back. The force of the ball sent the runner spread-eagle along the foul line.

The female base umpire raced over and shouted, "Out! You're out of the game. Get out," she shouted, pointing at Hank. "You're an animal."

"Look, blindy," yelling and pointing to his left leg, "he deliberately clipped me."

The umpire pointed toward the dugout, and she shouted back with eyes blazing, "You are out of the game!" She turned and walked away. Hank did not follow her.

Hank interrupted Jeff's thoughts. "We should award Rob a CMA certificate—an official member of the Certified Maniac Association."

But today was the day. In Jeff's pocket was an official search warrant approved by a U.S. Magistrate. Even if they lost Rob today, they would be back to search his house.

Rob, wearing a blue silk shirt, emerged at 8:21 a.m. with his companion. They entered the tan car and drove off. The tan car stopped at the plumbing outlet, and he gave her a peck on the cheek before she walked into the shop. So far, Rob had only run one stoplight.

Out to the rain-slick Beltway the tan car went. Rob was taking the same route he had taken so many times. The traffic was heavy. Hank kept his car close to Rob, not really worrying that they would be spotted. They had their search warrant today.

Rob's driving was a little better today because of the wet conditions. Hank was able to follow him for about eight miles down the Beltway. All of a sudden there were two tan Fords ahead. This situation had happened before. Two or three identical cars would appear ahead of them. They would eventually follow the wrong car.

Today was different. They followed Rob down an exit ramp from the Beltway. He entered a dirty, one-way street, going the wrong way. Two cars shot past, occupied by startled drivers.

Rob almost hit a light blue Honda Pilot, but it swerved at the last moment. Hank was not so lucky. This vehicle sideswiped Hank. Grinding shrieks of metal against metal filled the morning air.

Hank shouted, "You jerk!" and sped off after the tan car. The fenders rattled and the wheels shimmied as Hank gunned his old

Ford. Jeff closed his eyes and let the vibrating valves and rushing wind numb his fears.

Lady Luck had changed today. With a squeaking and groaning engine, Hank and Jeff were able to follow Rob. Rob parked at a moderately expensive apartment complex. He entered one of the apartments. A young girl greeted him at the door in a nightgown.

Jeff and Hank watched the apartment all morning. It was chilly, but the sun soon came out. Nothing happened. Suddenly Hank pointed. "There's the third one this morning!" Jeff knew what Hank was talking about. Hank had the habit of counting and pointing out people who were picking their nose in their car. People forget while they are in their cars that other drivers can see what they are doing.

At 12:30 p.m., Hank walked over to the local "greasy spoon" and brought back some Cokes and several hamburgers.

Halfway through his hamburger Hank asked, "Did you ever catch flies with your hands when you were a kid?"

"Catch flies?"

"I got to be the champion on my block. There's a secret to catching flies. You wait until the fly lands on a flat surface. You cup your hands like this." Hank cupped his hand in the shape of a U with his fingers together.

"Now slowly you put your hand about two feet in front of the fly—not in back of him. It's important that you are bold and not try to sneak up on him. You grab for him. Now he's going to fly, but if you are fast enough, he'll fly right into your hand."

"What do you do with him?"

"You throw him very hard against a hard surface. That'll kill him. I wonder if I could patent my hand?" Hank grinned as he admired his hand.

"Which are easier to catch, male or female flies?"

"Did you know that in Shekou, China," Hank ignored the question, "They eat snakes, vultures, and beetles? Owl or vulture soup apparently will cure a woman's headache. I needed that kind of soup with my ex."

"Do you want my hamburger? My headache would disappear if I had to eat vulture soup."

"I've been told that owl soup is good," Hank smiled.

At about 1:30 p.m., Rob and the young slender girl came out and went swimming in the blue-green-colored apartment pool. There was a fine mist rising from the heated pool. The young girl had on a bikini. Rob had on a wild, multi-colored swimming suit.

Jeff wrote down the address and apartment number. "Why don't we go back and check out his house now? I believe he'll be occupied for a while. Maybe we'll find something in his house that'll blow this clown out of the water"

Hank drove back toward Rob's brownstone and parked about a block from his entrance. "Not a good neighborhood for two white snoopers," Hank exclaimed. They watched the house for a few minutes. Then they walked up and knocked on the door. Several curious people walked past them.

No one answered. Jeff picked the lock, and they quickly entered. There is no Fifth Amendment prohibition in a tax case against a use of a search warrant to obtain incriminating records.

Jeff and Hank systematically searched the house. Jeff was the first one to find anything.

"Hank, here's some slips of paper. It's flash paper." Flash paper is the slips upon which the taker of the bets writes down the name of the bettor and the amount of the bet. It's flash paper so that in case of a raid, the slips can be set afire, and they will burn rapidly, without any ash, leaving no evidence. They also may use water-soluble rice paper.

"They must be involved in a bookmaking operation." A bookmaking operation is centered around some sporting event, whereas the numbers racket involves the selection of a random number.

Numbers operations use different ways of picking a winner. The last three digits in the daily "take" at a nearby race track could be the mechanism for picking the winner.

Some numbers rackets use the Federal Reserve Notes to select the winner. The number of Federal Reserve Notes printed per day is published in the next day's paper. The last three digits in the published amount is the winner for the previous day.

Both Jeff and Hank continued to search the house. Jeff heard Hank mumbling something. Jeff walked into the bedroom.

Hank was sitting in a chair in front of Rob's dresser. He was saying, "And this one is for running the stoplight! This one is for going the wrong way on the one-way street! This one is for wrecking my car!"

Hank had found a gross of multi-colored condoms. He was putting a small hole with a pin in each of the condoms. Hank looked up when Jeff entered. "That turkey is certainly not using these on his old lady. He must be living with that young girl. I hope he gets surprised!"

"You are bad, Hank." Jeff smiled.

They found nothing else of significance in the house. The search had been a snipe hunt. A few pieces of paper would hardly convince a hard-nosed judge.

Jeff and Hank drove back to the apartment. Rob's tan car was still parked in front of the apartment house.

They waited. It was not quite as cold as it was earlier. They played several hands of "21."

Rob exited from the apartment door around 5:30 p.m. He drove back to the plumbing outlet and picked up his old lady, and they stopped at a local fish joint and ate.

While watching them eat, Jeff said, "You know, she may be running the gambling racket out of the plumbing outlet. Rob may not be a runner. He may just be a gigolo."

They were both quiet for a while as they watched them eat. Finally Hank responded, "I'll find out who owns the plumbing outfit. Can you put a pen register on their phone?" Hank knew that Jeff had a telephone company friend who sometimes did some moonlighting for him.

They followed Rob home, and then they went back to IRS headquarters. There was a note on Jeff's desk to call Nick Anderson at his house. Jeff dialed Nick's home number. One of his kids answered the phone. Nick was cutting some firewood.

After a short while, an out-of-breath "Hello" sounded at the other end.

"Hi, Nick, this is Jeff Burke. You're going to have a heart attack cutting wood."

"It will be my wife's fault. She likes to use the fireplace. It lets more heat out of the chimney than it produces. The reason I called is that I have some information concerning Richard Onner."

After a short pause to yell at one of his kids, Nick continued.

"My supervisor is on me again."

"What is he hassling you about now?"

"He wants me to forget about Onner."

"Forget about Onner?" Jeff asked in surprise.

"Yeah, he claims our case production has fallen off, and he doesn't want us getting involved in anything that can't be closed quickly."

"Those damn supervisors. They don't care about quality. All they want are the numbers."

"You are right," replied Nick. "Would you meet me outside the office? I have to be near the British embassy tomorrow. Can you meet me at the north end of the parking lot at the Rock Creek Park around 4:00 p.m.?"

"Sure, see you there."

Jeff then called his friend who was a telephone repairman and asked him to bring a pen register and to meet him in front of the plumbing outlet at 9:00 that evening.

After eating some dinner, Jeff made his nightly unenthusiastic visit to the Flesher dumpster. Tonight was more productive. He found a stained five-dollar bill in the pocket of a discarded green shirt.

Jeff arrived at the plumbing outlet five minutes early and parked two blocks away. By the time he had strolled back to the building with his hands thrust deeply into his coat pockets, his friend was waiting with his toolbox near the building.

They walked around back and found the lead-in wire for the telephones inside the building. Within a short period of time, a pen register was attached to the appropriate wire.

The device would merely count the number of phone calls received by the phones in the building. A pen register was illegal without a court order. Any evidence gathered from this source could not be used in court. But if the plumbing outlet was receiving a large number of phone calls, this fact would help them decide whether to continue their investigation of Rob and his old lady. Bookies use the phone often in a bookmaking operation.

Jeff did not mind breaking the law a little bit when he was dealing with organized crime. The major source of revenue for organized crime was from illegal gambling. The second and third sources of revenue were loan sharking and narcotics. Jeff hoped he would be able to shut down the gambling racket in Baltimore.

Since 1960, the IRS had worked closely with the Justice Department to stop the menacing tentacles of organized crime. Jeff had been assigned to several Justice Department "strike forces" in past years. Jeff knew the extent to which organized crime had infiltrated legitimate businesses. The Gambino Mafia family is reputed to own control of the pizzeria industry in many areas of the East. This family is monopolizing the manufacture of mozzarella cheese. Such information was mind-boggling to the average citizen. Also, organized crime had even penetrated the Federal government; gambling, prostitution and bribery had been found by the FBI in the Interstate Commerce Commission, the Department of Housing and Urban Development, and Congress.

There is a nationwide alliance of at least twenty-four tightly knit Mafia families that controls organized crime in the United States. Their members are reputed to be Italians and Sicilians or of Italian or Sicilian descent. These families are linked together by agreements, and they obey a nine-member commission. This Mafia has infiltrated many legitimate businesses and labor unions. These liaisons give them power over officials at all levels of government.

Most large gambling is operated or controlled by organized crime members. The numbers racket can be described as a pyramid:

The player is not really a part of the organization, but starts the action by placing a bet with the first member of the organization—the runner or collector.

The runner works at locations that change from time to time, depending upon police operations. The runner may receive as much as 25% commission on the gross "play" for the day. Further, in some areas, the runner may withhold up to 10% of the winnings as a tip for himself.

Next in line is the pick-up. His function is to collect the day's "play" from the runner and transfer it either to the bank or to a "drop" where other pick-up men leave their day's "play." From the "drop" the money is moved to the bank. These pick-up men may work on a straight salary basis, which depends upon the locale or the volume of business.

The controller is next in line. He is the boss. He hires or fires employees, operates the office, and settles disputes between players and runners. His take may be as high as 35% of the gross from which he pays the runners about 25% and the pick-up men's salary.

The head master is the banker. He furnishes the capital for the operation, and he generally receives an accounting for his profits on a weekly basis. Since he is high up in the organized crime business, his name is protected.

Jeff's job, like the other Special Agents, was to disrupt illegal gambling by drastically reducing the profits by collecting taxes and penalties on such income which has not been reported and by prosecuting those who commit criminal tax violations. Aside from the income tax, there is an excise tax of 0.25% on wagering income and self-employment tax of 15.3%. Also, there is an occupational tax of $500 on all persons engaged in accepting wagers. One problem is that a large group of citizens regard many of these crimes as minor vices since they do not hurt anyone, except the IRS.

Once the pen register was attached, Jeff paid his friend fifty dollars. His last remark was "You don't know me."

As Jeff drove home, the wind was gusting over Baltimore. As he got close to his parking lot, he was thinking about the number of unanswered questions about his case. He thought about the twelve billion dollars wagered annually on Bingo—the real global sport. There are 63 million players worldwide—3 million in England alone. Online Bingo is becoming quite popular. The state lotteries were coming along fast, however.

Chapter 7

If Thomas Jefferson thought taxation without representation was bad, he should see how it is with representation.
— Rush Limbaugh

A person poured nine ounces of methanol mixed with nitromethane and 25% castor oil into the gas tank of the model airplane. The castor oil is used as a lubricant because it doesn't burn like petroleum oil. The methanol/nitromethane mix is similar to the fuel used in the fast race cars.

The red, white, and blue airplane had a five-foot wingspread and was powered by a six cubic-inch displacement Japanese-made engine. The model plane was made of balsa wood, covered with silk. "Snoopy," a white beagle wearing a yellow hat, sat in the cockpit.

The model plane was controlled with a radio transmitter on the ground. The controls on the radio transmitter are basically identical to the controls in an actual airplane. Channels control the throttle, rudder, elevators, and ailerons. Model airplanes may fly as fast as two hundred miles per hour.

Once in the air the plane spun and turned, looped, and dipped. In the air the plane took on a different perspective. Although the model plane could only reach a top altitude of three hundred feet, it looked like a full-sized airplane flying at three thousand feet.

Buzz-zz. Buzz-zz-zz. Around and around the plane flew. The performance of the plane would have thrilled any of the 300,000 members of the Academy of Model Aeronautics.

* * *

Jeff had followed Rob again this morning. He followed him on the Beltway but lost him. He drove to the apartment and Rob's car

was parked there. Around 11:30 a.m. Rob and his girlfriend came
outside to swim. Jeff went back to his cluttered office. In the corner on his coat rack was a wrinkled red tie and his temporarily retired Sentry Superstars softball cap.

The morning mail brought the information about Onner's bank
deposits from his two Martinsburg bank accounts. Jeff prepared a
bank deposit analysis on Onner. The bank deposit method looks at
the funds deposited during the year. This method attempts to re-
construct gross taxable receipts rather than adjusted income. As he
had suspected, this analysis did not disclose any significant unreported income.

Total deposits to all accounts	$95,000
Less: Transfers and re-deposits	2,100
= Net Deposits	92,900
Plus: Cash Expenditures	6,800
= All total receipts	99,700
Less: Funds known from sources	98,600
= Funds from unknown sources	$ 1,100

Jeff did notice that the bank symbols "EC" appeared twice on
the bank statements. This symbol indicates an Exchange Charge
for converting foreign currency into U.S. dollars, or a charge for a
cable or transmittal costs. Jeff needed to determine the source of such
foreign monies in order to determine its taxability.

Jeff knew that some U.S. taxpayers obtain a Canadian bank account which is payable in U.S. dollars. Such a technique circum-
vents the Supreme Court's ruling that a bank owns the depositor's
records, and a bank is required to release such records to the IRS
at any time without warrant. For payments the taxpayer does not
wish the IRS to know about, he avoids his U.S. bank account. He
can buy money orders from many different places and pay such
amounts.

Also, Onner regularly was using his safe deposit boxes. For the
three-year period, Onner had entered one or the other box approximately once a week, normally on Monday. This factor may
or may not be significant. The Federal Reserve Bank of Boston has

estimated that Americans hoard more than $50 billion in cash, with 40% of this figure in $100 bills. Most hoards are under one thousand dollars.

There was some good news. His supervisor indicated that a U.S. District Court dismissed a couple's claim against Jeff and another Revenue Agent. The couple had asserted that Jeff and the other agent over assessed them due to their personal dislike of them. The judge ordered the couple to pay the legal costs for Jeff and the other agent. "Now there's a good judge," Jeff smiled ruefully, when he heard the news.

Next, Jeff went through the newspaper clippings accumulated by his secretary and administrative aide. They clipped articles from several papers that might indicate lavish spenders or unreported wealth. A lavish wedding party, an individual appearing on a television quiz show, jewelry on the wife of a prominent citizen, a couple embarking on an expensive vacation, a reported theft of a large sum of money, a sale of a valuable piece of property or other items in the local paper that might lead to a fraud investigation. Today's clippings were not promising. The clippings of several marriages of well-to-do families and announcements of two store openings were thrown in his special round receptacle.

Jeff made several notes to follow up on one item. A private citizen had found $10,000 buried in a vacant lot on the West Side of Baltimore. An internal memo was written to check next year to see if this fine citizen reported the income. Yes, even money that is found is taxable. Also, Jeff would check with the police in several weeks to see if anyone claimed the money. He also would check on the owner of the vacant lot.

One other item showed some promise. In the obituary column was a notice that Albert D'Estang had died. D'Estang was suspected by many to be a member of organized crime. Jeff filled out Form 4298, Audit Requisition and Information Report, which is used by an agent when he uncovers information or leads relating to estate or gift tax filing requirements. The purpose of the form is to inform district personnel to examine the underground figure. Only with cooperation between Revenue Agents and Estate Tax Examiners will individual income tax returns of an organized crime suspect, together with any estate tax return, be subjected to a coordinated in-depth examination. The operation of organized crime is highly vulnerable with the death of a major figure.

Hunches and newspaper reports often lead to conviction. A story is told to young agents about one particular conviction. Apparently, a supervisor of a Fraud Squad found things to be slack. The supervisor picked the names of ten pharmacists from the telephone directory and sent out agents at random to audit their returns. One of the taxpayers ended up in a criminal case.

With his paperwork under control and several telephone messages returned, Jeff left his office to meet Nick at Rock Creek Park. On the way to the parking lot, Jeff stopped at the "Check This" bulletin board. One bulletin board had been set aside for humorous and sometimes profane letters and responses from taxpayers. Jeff's favorite was a letter in which a taxpayer had sent one turnip. Still on the bulletin board was a Form 1040 covered with red spots. Typed at the bottom of the form was the following caption:

"I have nothing left. Here is some blood. I hope you are satisfied!"

Aside from the usual obscenities, taxpayers were continually sending in fake forms with such signatures as Mickey Mouse, Benedict Arnold, Son of Sam, Al Capone, I. M. Ripoff, John Wilkes Booth, George Bush, and I No Pay. Often these anonymous jokers included play money.

Jeff had read in the paper several days ago about a university student who filed a lawsuit in defense of his right to scribble comments on the envelopes in which he mailed his monthly utility payment. The student indicated that he included the obscenities on the envelope to ridicule, express scorn for, and encourage public awareness of the unreasonable, unjust and unfair profit structure of the utility company. Jeff was sure that the IRS received more obscenities than any other organization.

One agent in the Baltimore office had been subjected to some unusual cruelty by a practical joker last year. For one week, an anonymous prankster deluged the agent with visitors and items he did not ask for—a piano, a burial vault, plumbers, carpet installers, an ambulance crew responding to a false report of a heart attack, and a 65th birthday retirement party. A load of manure was unceremoniously dumped on his driveway. The parade of workers at the agent's home and office included a pest exterminator who said he was told "there was a lot of rats up here on this floor."

Obviously, IRS agents are not the most popular people around. One former IRS Commissioner indicated that "on the whole, the IRS has taken its lumps stoically, knowing full well that this is the lot of the tax collector. Indeed, the Bible offers cases of tax collectors being stoned to death, so in this light we are not doing too badly. Jesus did befriend Zacchaeus, the chief tax collector, after he climbed a sycamore tree."

During Jeff's second year as an IRS Agent, a self-employed truck driver had unleashed his German shepherd and allowed it to attack Jeff. The damage: 26 stitches on Jeff's left arm and 12 stitches on his right leg.

The truck driver was arrested and released on a $2,500 personal recognizance bond. The felonious assault charge carried a maximum penalty of $5,000 and three years in prison. Apparently, the judge did not like IRS agents either. The truck driver was fined $1,000 and was out on a one-year suspended jail sentence.

Jeff noticed a new addition to the bulletin board today. A taxpayer had sent in a small bag of hair with the following cryptic message:

> I am pleased to enclose the hair which I tore from my head while trying to fill out my 1040 Form. Would someone try to simplify this form before I become bald?" Did you know that President Franklin Delano Roosevelt once said, 'I am wholly unable to figure out the amount of my tax as this is a problem in higher mathematics?' He asked the IRS to determine the amount he owed.

Chuckling as he went to the parking lot, Jeff got into his car. Jeff drove toward Washington to meet Nick at Rock Creek Park. The CB

radio chatter was hot and heavy today. Smokey the Bear was out trying to collect his dinner money. As one taxpayer told Jeff, only
truckers and rednecks have CBs today. Cell phones destroyed this
market. Oh well, he still has one, and as the country-western song
says, "they can kiss my glass."

Jeff had brought his CB to break the monotony and alert him to
traffic snarls. Radar detectors were illegal in Virginia and D.C., so his
Escort was in the trunk. But other than truckers, few people had CB
radios today. Most young people did not know what a CB was. However, today he avoided two "bear bites" by slowing down after being
alerted by two anonymous CBers. The first warning was humorous:

> Smile and comb your hair. There's a Smokey in the grass
> by the airport exit, and he's taking pictures.

Jeff immediately slowed to "double nickels." Jeff's handle was
"Super Snooper," compliments of a previous girlfriend.

Both Nick and Jeff drove into the parking lot at Rock Creek Park
at about the same time. Jeff walked over to Nick's car and said,
"Why don't we talk in the park?" Nick was fidgeting with his pipe.

Once they were walking Nick began talking. "As I mentioned,
my supervisor wants me to cool it with Onner. But I did get one more
piece of information. Some time ago, the Washington office was
concerned about the use of secret Swiss bank accounts by U.S. tax
evaders. You may remember that caper. But the Swiss banks sent the
account holders their bank statements in plain envelopes. Several
agents wrote the Swiss banks about opening accounts and noted
the postal meter numbers on the replies.

Buzz-zz-zz. Nick paused as he looked at the model plane flying
to their left.

"Anyway, the IRS used high-speed copiers at several large post
offices to copy fronts of all airmail letters arriving from Switzerland in plain envelopes. Next these letters were checked against the
banks' meter numbers. A list of several thousand probable account
holders was compiled. I went through the list and found Onner's
name. Richard Onner has a Swiss bank account," Nick almost
shouted.

They had walked up to a small stream. There was a long pause as Nick filled his pipe and lit it. They turned around and began walking toward the parking lot. Buzz-zz-zz. The plane was still flying.

Jeff seemed reflective. Finally he said, "Well, I prepared a bank deposit analysis on him and he was okay. If he does have a Swiss bank account, he must have a great deal of unreported income. Do you have any theories on how he is getting the money?"

"Nope." Nick frowned slightly. "He is not dealing directly with taxpayers. Could he be screwing around with the computer programs? Maybe he is eliminating taxpayers from the master files for a fee."

An IRS agent dealing with taxpayers was in a better position to extort payoffs than someone like Onner. An agent can subject taxpayers to illegal surveillance and investigation to obtain payoffs or blackmail money. There had been situations of illegal payoffs or blackmail by agents. Such situations were, of course, in violation of federal income tax laws.

Jeff thought the model plane was close. He looked to his right in time to see the plane coming directly at them. "Watch out!" he shouted.

At the same time, Jeff dove for the shelter of a large rock. Crash! The plane hit Nick on his right side. Jeff heard Nick's agonizing scream. The impact was so forceful that it drove the shaft of the plane through the body's main organs. Then there was a loud explosion.

Jeff was in a long eerie tunnel filled with light. He felt himself leaving his body. Jeff was floating above the park watching the pandemonium unfold below.

He saw two bodies lying on the ground. His body was lying behind a large rock. Nick's distorted body was still. Nick's body was black from the explosion. Blood and methanol/nitromethane were flowing freely on the ground. His pipe was broken into two pieces, lying about 15 feet from his lifeless mesh of body and plane.

Two ambulances arrived. Jeff watched his body being placed on a stretcher and slid into the first ambulance. Nick's body was placed into the second ambulance.

Jeff awoke from his nightmare world hearing the sound of a loud siren. At the hospital, the doctor in the emergency room decided

that Jeff only had a mild concussion. This discovery did not help
the ringing in his ears or the soreness in his right shoulder where
he had hit the ground.

Chapter 8

What always happens—what has happened in every nation that has ever set up a graduated income tax—is that the highest actual rates are paid by the middle class.

—from "The April Game"

Jeff learned that Nick was pronounced dead on arrival at the hospital.

Jeff spent the night in the hospital and was released the next morning. He was lucky. The rock had shielded him from the blast, but his ears were still ringing. The dive behind the rock had not helped his prior injury.

The investigating detective came to the hospital Friday. He told Jeff that after the impact of the model plane, there had been an explosion. A plastic explosive device had been taped to the plane. A radio transmitter on the ground had detonated the device.

The detective had been unable to get a description of the operator of the model plane. The operator had disappeared immediately after the explosion. But a strand of blonde hair was found in a crack in a piece of the destroyed model plane.

Jeff had a blank listlessness on Friday and Saturday. He did go to Nick's wake Saturday morning. He stayed only about 20 minutes. It was depressing. What could he say to Nick's wife and his children?

He did see Nick's supervisor at the wake, and asked him to send him a list of Nick's informers. In case of an accident or suspicious death, a group supervisor is allowed to check the informers of an agent. The group supervisor indicated that he would send Jeff a list of these people.

Jeff intended to check out each of these informers. One of them might have a clue to Nick's killer. Or one of them might be the killer.

While in the hospital, Jeff had gone through several Baltimore and Washington newspapers. Jeff noted that there was a regional meeting of the Academy of Model Aeronautics at the Washington Hilton next Friday and Saturday. The person who killed Nick might be attending this meeting.

After lunch on the next Friday, Jeff was at the Hilton. The lobby was filled with people with AMA nametags. Here and there were some Hilton employees with their "We Care" buttons.

Ironically, the lobby was also filled with CPAs. IRS agents and CPAs were natural adversaries. There are more than 370,000 CPAs in 128 countries, many of whom belong to the AICPA. Bob Newhart started out as an accountant, and Milton Mostel (elder brother of Zero Mostel) was a sole practitioner. A former chief executive of Chrysler was a CPA. The conservative society of CPAs was holding their annual convention and vacation in Washington.

Jeff obtained a list of the people who registered for the AMA convention. Even though this was a Northeast regional meeting of the AMA there were a number of individuals from the states outside the Northeast.

For a glimpse at his "Special Agent" card with the eagle and the wording "Special Agent, U.S. Treasury, Internal Revenue Service, Intelligence," Jeff easily obtained a free name tag from the lady registering members.

> Hi, I'm
> Jeff Burke
> Academy of Model Aeronautics

A faint smile flickered on her face when he told her that he was checking up on the AICPA group. He asked for her cooperation and silence. Even without looking at the name tags on the people in the hotel, Jeff could tell who were accountants and who were

AMA members. Some of the accountants were dressed in their dark, pinstriped suits, and the AMA members were dressed in more casual attire.

Social organizations, non-profit country clubs, and similar social clubs are generally not taxable. Exemption from taxation is granted to such organizations if they are organized and operated for pleasure, recreation, and other non-profit purposes. But the net earnings of the organization must not inure to the benefit of any private stockholder or member. Also, the corporate income tax is imposed upon any unrelated business income of exempt organizations. So Jeff could have been legitimately checking on either of the organizations.

Jeff milled around the hotel lobby for a while and drifted in and out of several lectures on aeronautics on the mezzanine level. Most of the model airplane devotees were glued to their seats, attentive to each word from the speaker's lips.

The largest group was in the Presidential Ballroom. Jeff walked into the room and sat down under a magnificent chandelier. The foil-colored wallpaper was covered with what looked to be either Christmas wreaths or snowflakes. Along the top of the wall were eagles holding a shield, an olive branch, and an arrow. There were stars around the edges of the ceiling on gold velvet. On the front wall were several large smudge-free bright mirrors.

The podium at the front had Capital Hilton written on it, with a picture of the top of the Capitol. A rangy, raw-boned man was behind the podium starting to talk about radio controlled helicopters.

"Remember, airplanes want to fly, helicopters don't."

That's a profound statement, Jeff thought.

"You must do eight different things all at the same time," continued the speaker.

Jeff got up and left. He was tempted to tell the speaker to buy an octopus to fly the helicopter.

Once outside the Presidential Ballroom, Jeff thought, "Maybe I should go to some of the CPA's lectures and learn the latest tax avoidance schemes." Feeling at loose ends, Jeff went into the Rogue's

Manor, a small lounge inside the hotel. Jeff sat down at a small table and ordered a Bloody Mary. Jeff thought, "How do you find a killer when your only piece of evidence is one strand of hair?"

"Hi, Jeff," came an intriguing voice from the table next to him. "So this is how you miss all of those boring lectures," her voice continued in pleasant tones.

A strawberry blonde encased in a navy suit with a white blouse was smiling at him. She was in her late thirties.

Jeff gulped and responded, "Hello. How are you?" As soon as the words were out, Jeff knew his response was not very original. He did not recognize the speaker.

"I read your name tag. I was bored myself with the speakers. Hope you don't mind me being so bold. May I join you?"

"Sure," mumbled Jeff. Jeff read her name tag, Deidre Moore, as she moved to his table.

"Are you a model airplane nut?" Jeff asked, smiling.

"Yes, for about four years. I went through the typical housewife vocations: bridge club, African violet club, and needlework group. I was bored. So I got into the local model airplane club."

"I have a scale model of a World War I Fokker D-7. It cost almost $900. I love to fly it. Watching my plane fly is really an experience rather than a spectator sport. What do you do?"

"I'm a businessman," Jeff lied.

"I'm married," Deidre continued. "My husband is a doctor. A doctor of philosophy, that is. He is a professor. He teaches psychology."

"Professors don't get paid much. He could make more money collecting garbage in New York City or some other major city. Many students spend ten years obtaining degrees after high school and wind up driving taxis."

"Can you imagine an English or Math Ph.D. driving a cab? There are too many Ph.D.s for the available jobs. Why, the other day I read in the paper that a new postmaster in Snook, Texas, makes $57,000 per year. Now Snook has a population of less than 1,000 people. The article indicated that the total receipts from the Snook post office were less than $20,000. Probably one-half of the professors in such disciplines as English, Political Science, and Economics make less than most postmasters with only a high school education. A teacher on strike in Wisconsin can make at least $100,000."

"That's probably why postage stamps are so high," said Jeff quickly. He could not believe it. Was he being picked up? What should he do, Jeff thought, as he tried to control his anxiety.

There was a moment of silence before Deidre continued. "Most people don't realize it, but many professors work fifty or sixty hours per week. Bill, of course, enjoys his work. He does have flexible hours. But he just works too much. He complains that with grade inflation and coursework deflation, students do not study anymore. They pay their fees and get their Bs."

She paused and looked at Jeff. "I helped him do one interesting experiment dealing with the subconscious. Most of us react to certain symbols without our knowledge. My husband does some experiments in a behavioral lab on campus. There is a machine there, which measures the heart's action, brain waves, and perspiration. If he hooked you up to this machine and flashed pictures or signs on a screen, you would react, possibly violently, to certain symbols. This reaction is subconscious."

"A picture of a witch can make an individual react violently. All those machines would go wild. Or a male might react violently if a picture of a woman executive smoking a cigar is flashed on the screen."

"Billy indicates that a great deal of research went into the selection of the ear of corn on a famous package of corn flakes. This image caused mothers to go over and pick up a box of cereal without even knowing why."

"Similar research was conducted with Mr. Clean, the baldheaded fellow, who advertised a laundry product many years ago. Apparently, his image caused women to pick up his bottle."

"Do you know what subliminal suggestions are?" Deidre asked as her light blue eyes probed his confused hazel eyes.

As Jeff nodded yes, Deidre answered her own question. "A subliminal suggestion is a message flashed on a screen at a speed too fast for conscious reading. The television industry outlawed subliminal suggestions years ago. You may remember a *Columbo* episode some years ago dealing with subliminal suggestions."

"My husband used subliminal suggestions to improve the grades of students. He randomly divided each undergraduate class into two groups—a control group and an experimental group.

"At the beginning of each class, he showed the experimental group subliminally the message: MY MOMMY AND I ARE ONE."

"Mommy and I are one?" Jeff responded with a puzzled look.

"Yes," she said, removing Jeff's pen from his charcoal grey coat pocket. "It looked like this." She quickly scribbled MY MOMMY AND I ARE ONE on the cocktail napkin that had formerly been under her drink.

"Do the capital letters mean anything?"

"No, I don't think so. The second section of each group was shown this message." Deidre again scribbled on the napkin: PEOPLE ARE WALKING.

"What does that do?" asked Jeff.

"Nothing. PEOPLE ARE WALKING is supposed to be a neutral message." Although both messages were flashed on the screen at high speeds, the messages did register on the unconscious minds of the students.

"Would you believe that the experimental group of students earned significantly higher grades in class than the control group who saw the neutral message? The difference in grades was approximately ten points out of one hundred." Deidre returned the pen.

Jeff was seriously interested in the conversation. "Why did their grades improve?"

"Well, at an early age we develop a conflict with our image of our mother—actually, a love/hate relationship," continued Deidre quickly.

"We like our mother because she is the source of all our comfort, nourishment, and security. During this symbiotic stage we develop a sense of oneness with our mother. But mother cannot cuddle us forever. She stops breastfeeding us and fondling us. We resent this lack of attention."

"In self-defense we suppress these two conflicting feelings. The more inner conflict an individual has, the better his grades can be improved by sending a message, which reactivates this feeling of oneness."

"The message MY MOMMY AND I ARE ONE through subliminal stimulation has a comforting effect. It allows an individual to perform better than normal."

"Surprisingly, the message must be shown subliminally. This same message shown supraliminally has no effect on the individual. Only when an individual's awareness is bypassed can this message have an effect."

"What's the difference between subliminal and supraliminal?" asked Jeff.

"When it's subliminal it's shown too fast for the eye to be able to recognize the message; but when it's supraliminal, you can read it."

"Remember Son of Sam—the New York killer who prowled the streets during 1977 randomly killing people? He had no knowledge about his mother. Maybe that's why he was hearing voices telling him to kill."

"My husband found that people closer to schizophrenia showed a greater improvement in grades. You know what a schizophrenic is, don't you? That's an individual with bizarre delusions. Such an individual has more inner conflict."

"Probably both the control and experimental groups had grade increases," Jeff said, tasting his drink for the first time since this conversation started.

"Placebo is Latin for 'I shall please.' It refers to an inactive substance or procedure used with a patient under the pretense of an effective treatment. A patient receives a pill, which may contain only milk sugar. If the patient believes the pill is a powerful drug, it may work."

Deidre paused for a moment as if she were turning the page of her lecture notes and sipped at her drink. Jeff glanced at his watch and with some hesitation asked, "Is this your first visit to Washington, D.C.?"

"It has been many years since I've been here. Would you do me a favor? We are only two blocks from the White House. Would you like to take a tour of it? I have two tickets."

"Sure, why not." Jeff was glad to get up. His body had shifted into a position where he was hurting. Besides, Jeff had never toured the White House even though he had been in Washington many times.

The walk to the White House through Lafayette Park was short. There was a brisk wind blowing, so they were thankful that there were only a few people waiting to enter on the side of the White House. They had to pass through a six-foot-tall chain-link fence, which had been built in the early nineties. Deidre and Jeff walked slowly along the glass-enclosed colonnade to the ground floor corridor where Jeff saw portraits of Eleanor Roosevelt, Jacqueline Kennedy Onassis, and Lady Bird Johnson. One of the three Regency chandeliers sparkled on a selection of Presidential china displayed in a Sheraton-style bookcase, which was made in Baltimore in 1803. On the top shelf, in the center, were plates used by George Washington at Mount Vernon.

Jeff was impressed with the 10-foot portrait of Chester Arthur, the 21st president. Jeff had never heard of him. Jeff saw the white busts of Abraham Lincoln and Christopher Columbus.

Jeff and Deidre spoke little as they leisurely made their way through the walking tour. Jeff looked into the library on the right of the corridor. The paneling of a soft grey color was broken by built-in bookcases and several paintings of Indians.

The Vermeil Room did not impress Jeff, but the velvet-lined cabinets, silk taffeta draperies, and the colorful English rug made the China Room a sight to see. One of the many tour guides, or maybe they were guards, pointed to the portrait of Mrs. Calvin Coolidge and said, "President Coolidge was scheduled to sit for the artist, Howard Christy, but the President was too preoccupied that day with events concerning the Teapot Dome oil scandal. The president postponed his appointment, and Mrs. Coolidge posed instead."

Flanking the portrait were Chippendale side chairs used by President George Washington in his earlier presidential residences.

Next they climbed the stairs to four state reception rooms and the State Dining Room. The Diplomatic reception room had panoramic wallpaper with scenes of the Natural Bridge of Virginia, Niagara Falls, New York Bay, West Point, and Boston Harbor. A tour guide indicated that the Map Room was used by Franklin Roosevelt as a situation room to follow the course of World War II.

The Green Room with its green watered-silk fabric wall and striped beige, green, and coral satin draperies was too green. The multi-colored carpet was worn. A painting on the far wall looked like some kind of strange, giant insect. The portrait, entitled "The Mosquito Net," was a woman sleeping in bed, covered by a black mosquito net.

Jeff liked the oval Blue Room. A portrait of John Adams hung on the west wall near a beautiful white marble mantel. The blue satin draperies with handmade fringe and gold satin valances and the Bellange Bergere armchairs were handsomely offset by the light beige wallpaper with a blue frieze around the top and bottom which was derived from classical motifs.

With only a glance into the Red Room, Jeff walked over to observe the State Dining Room with the gold damask draperies and a large portrait of Abraham Lincoln above a carved white mantel. The family dining room was unimpressive.

Jeff walked down the bright red carpet on Cross Hall toward the North Entrance Hall. He wondered if the portrait of President Truman at the west end of the hall was intentionally separated from the portrait of President Eisenhower at the east end. After glancing at the portraits of Presidents John Kennedy, Ronald Reagan, and George Bush, Jeff walked back downstairs. Deidre was still looking in the Red Room, chatting with one of the guides.

Downstairs Jeff purchased an inexpensive softback copy of *The White House: A Historical Guide*. Deidre was waiting near the doors at the North Entrance by the time Jeff walked back to the front.

"Well, what do you think about the place?" asked Deidre.

"It looks somewhat old and worn, especially some of the car-
pets. It doesn't fit my image of the home of the most powerful person in the world."

"Did you hear the guide say the place has six floors? President
Keeney and his family live on two floors. They only have 57 rooms."

"That's bigger than my apartment."

"By the way, did you notice the museum we passed coming down
here? It's the museum for the Treasury Building. There's still some
time before it closes. Would you like to see it?"

"Sure, why not," Jeff replied. Jeff hoped she did not notice the
slight blush on his face. The Treasury Department was his employer.

The Treasury Exhibit Hall was small. Immediately inside the
door was a bronzed bulletin board with the names of Treasury
Agents killed in the line of duty. There were two numismatic sales
counters open. Jeff bought a one and one-half inch pewter disc.
Deidre used a coin press and struck a medal showing the White
House on the obverse and the Presidential seal on the reverse.

When Deidre passed under the TV screen, which showed a picture of her, Jeff noticed her trying to arrange her blonde hair. Next
to this TV was a mannequin wearing a Fort Knox guard uniform
holding a machine gun.

There was an animated display of sculptors' art, a moonshine
still, some U.S. Customs artifacts, and a replica of a 1792 screw
coin press. Jeff was looking at a Lienhard transfer and engraving
machine when he heard Deidre laugh.

"Jeff, come over here. As a—," she paused—"businessman, you
should enjoy this song." She pointed to a piece of paper in a glass
display.

It was a song written in the 1920s, entitled "Tax, Tax, Tax":

> We are living in the days of war taxation. Its effect is felt
> by every occupation. There's a tax on things we drink and
> a tax on thoughts we think. It's causing lots of trouble and
> vexation. Such a Tax, Tax, Tax. Quite enough to break our
> backs on furniture and picture shows, furs, and drugs and

silken hose. Tax, Tax, and Tax. If you fondle your wife and get kisses a plenty, you'll pay four cents on all over twenty. Kiss goodbye to all your greenbacks. You're paying Tax, Tax, and Tax.

"There's a lot of truth in that old song," Jeff said when he finished skimming the words.

"We better get out of here. They're about to close," Deidre said, looking at her petite Rolex watch.

From the Treasury Building they walked down New York Avenue. It was beginning to get dark.

"Would you like to find a cab and go to a restaurant and eat?" Jeff asked.

"Yes! There's an Italian restaurant on the corner of M Street."

Jeff and Deidre engaged in some chitchat in the cab ride to the restaurant and while waiting for the food.

The food was adequate. After the meal they drifted down M Street toward the Hilton.

Across the street from the Hilton, Deidre stopped in front of Archibald's. It was "Washington's 1st Completely Topless Dancing Girls."

"Can you imagine," said Deidre, "only three blocks from the White House." She smiled. "Would you buy me a drink? I've never been in a topless dancing place."

As Jeff opened the door to let Deidre in, he noticed a large sign on the window of the establishment next door: "Quiche." In very small letters underneath was "carryout food."

As they made their way to a table on the first floor in the dimly lit long room, Jeff noticed a girl with red hair dancing on one of the two stages in front of the mirror. Jeff noticed that there were smudges and fingerprints on the mirror. The dancer was near the end of her act because she was down to her G-string. Jeff helped Deidre remove her coat and placed it on the back of her chair.

A bar went down the entire left side of the long room. The entire back wall was covered with mirrors. By the time they had gotten their drinks, the girl was finishing her act. She put on a thin nightgown and became a waitress.

Then a very tall woman got up from a table where she was sitting with a man who looked like a fullback for the Denver Broncos.

With the song "You Satisfy My Desires" as background, she began her performance. When she reached the G-string stage, one of the customers near the stage wrapped a bill, probably $5, around her string.

When Jeff had finished his first beer, he leaned over and whispered, "What did you think about her performance?"

Deidre merely smiled. After a few moments she leaned toward Jeff and took his hand. "One thing I forgot to tell you about the subliminal experiment, which I talked about earlier," she whispered. "It is possible to lower the performance of individuals. By using messages such as DESTROY MOTHER, KILL MOTHER, or SHOOT MOTHER, an individual's performance can be decreased. Do you think these messages would decrease your performance?"

Jeff did not respond. He was thinking that a certain softball may have decreased his performance. Was he up to it?

There were three young men sitting at the table next to Jeff. Jeff noticed that the dancer smiled at the table. He heard one of the men say excitedly, "She's smiling at me!"

"No, she's not. She's smiling at me," responded one of the other men.

After a second drink they left. When they got to the busy lobby, there was an awkward pause. "Would you like to get another drink in the bar?"

"No, I would rather talk. Why don't we go to my room."

The hotel room appeared to be recently redecorated. It smelled of perfume. Just like the movies, Deidre excused herself and went to the bathroom to change into something more comfortable.

Jeff awoke the next morning. At first he did not know where he was. But Deidre was not there. She had taken his copy of The White House and his pen.

A note was on the table with a grapefruit and a Danish pastry on a tray.

Jeff,

I had to leave early. Thank you.

Have breakfast on me.

"D"

It was late and Jeff remembered his diet. He ate the grapefruit, drank the orange juice, ignored the coffee and pastry, and left the hotel room.

Jeff hung around the hotel lobby for about an hour, but he could not find Deidre. He checked the front desk, but she had already checked out. He wrote down her address: 1112 Broad Street, Kent, Ohio, 44242 from the AMA attendance list.

As Jeff left the hotel, he noticed a blonde hair on his coat. "What the heck," Jeff thought, "I'll let the detective check out this strand of hair for the fun of it. I will see how accurate he is in the information he can give me about Deidre." Jeff placed it in a small envelope and put it in his breast pocket.

Buzz-Buzz—Jeff instinctively turned his head toward the sound. His hands were shaking. The noise was merely a cell phone in a parked automobile on the street. Someone was trying to reach the occupant, who was missing.

It was a reminder to Jeff that he had to find the model plane operator. Who was he? How could he find him? Even the dreary, drizzly day could not upset his cheerful spirits.

A small article appeared in the Sunday *Washington Post*. Apparently, a maid had died from food poisoning at the Hilton on Saturday. Jeff did *not* notice the article in the newspaper.

Chapter 9

Proper income tax reform is simple to define: It's closing all your loopholes, while leaving open mine.

—L. A. Mason

It was Saturday evening. Commissioner Jimmy Callaway did not expect to have an exciting evening. He and his wife, Betty, were ringing the doorbell of the Cranfords. Harry Cranford was the Press Secretary of the President.

Jane Cranford opened the door. "Hi, Betty. How are you, Jimmy?" Betty and Jane had been close friends for a number of years. Jane was quite attractive and affluent. She had a long aristocratic nose and her lips were light pink.

"Jimmy, Harry's in the living room."

Jimmy walked into the living room. The card table was already placed in the middle of the room. Today would be one of those infrequent times in which Jimmy would be in a situation in which he felt insecure.

Jimmy did not like to play bridge. In fact, he couldn't play bridge that well. He never had time in college to learn the game.

He was a dummy player. He played so that he would be the dummy hand. The dummy is the player who must expose his hand, and the declarer plays the exposed hand in addition to his own hand.

Jimmy was careful never to introduce a new suit. Jimmy could never keep track of the cards that had been played. He never worried whether the "Jack of Spades" had been played until he lost a trick and his wife would sit erect and peer fiercely across the table. He tried never to be the declarer.

Let his wife play the hand. She was good! Why not, that was all she did. That, and shop, and spend money.

"Hello, Jimmy. How are you tonight?" Harry interrupted Jimmy's thoughts.

Harry was a large-framed man over six feet in height. His facial features were sharp. His straight, black hair fell over his forehead, with long descending sideburns. He always wore black-rimmed glasses. Harry was an avid tennis player.

During the Eisenhower era, it was golf. For Nixon it was bowling. Johnson had pulled dogs' ears. Ford had played golf and skied. Carter played tennis and softball. Reagan cut wood and rode horses. George Bush (41st) boated. Clinton jogged. George Bush (43rd) jogged and cut wood. Obama played basketball and golfed. The current President carried on the tennis tradition.

Jimmy did not especially like Harry Cranford. Harry was too liberal. As a college student Harry had been an active member of the Americans for Democratic Action. Harry carried this leftward tilt into his current job as Press Secretary.

He was, however, one of the three or four close advisors to the President. For this reason alone, Jimmy always kept a civil demeanor while around Harry. Jimmy did know how to smile.

"Oh, pretty good, I suppose," replied Jimmy. Jimmy knew there would be five minutes of social conversation and the wives would be ready for combat.

"Is a whiskey okay?" asked Harry.

"Sure."

True to form, in five minutes they were seated around the table. Betty had won the bid and Jimmy was the dummy hand.

The only advantage that Jimmy had over Harry was that Jimmy could get Harry into a political discussion. Harry would then screw up.

"Harry, did you notice in the *Wall Street Journal* yesterday that the Chinese have gained parity with the United States in its total nuclear striking capacity? A recently issued study indicates that the U.S. has only a 30% advantage in its arsenal of intercontinental nuclear missiles and bombers. They are catching up with us in space, also."

"Why do you read that right-wing rag? The article probably did not mention overkill. Do you know that China could destroy every American with a personal force of 25 tons of TNT?" Harry asked sharply.

"Harry, I'm talking about delivery of destructive force. It does no good if the bombs are sitting on the ground when China attacks us. You know Carter killed the B-1 bomber in 1977. Then he had the guts to give away the Panama Canal."

Harry over-trumped his wife. That was an embarrassing mistake. His wife groaned. Harry tried to retrieve the card, but she said mockingly, "A card laid is a card played. Keep your mind on the game, Harry!"

But Harry continued. "Plutonium is the basic material needed to make fission, or the atomic bomb. It is also used as a trigger for the much more powerful thermonuclear bombs. To make a bomb it takes less than ten pounds of pure plutonium or about eighteen pounds of plutonium extracted from the spent uranium fuel or approximately twenty-two pounds of plutonium oxide."

"So for that reason Carter tried to cancel the fast-breeder reactor at Oak Ridge, Tennessee," responded Jimmy crisply. "Why, the risks associated with the Clinch River reactor are manageable, and the project would turn fission energy into an unlimited resource. We are running out of energy."

"Look, Carter was trying to curb the production of plutonium around the world. Do you realize the exposure of nuclear facilities against dangers of attack, sabotage, and hijacking? Why, in the late '70s, one intelligence agency discovered that 8,000 pounds of weapons-grade nuclear material was diverted from the power plant."

Harry paused and threw down a four of spades and then continued. "Jimmy, each year the odds increase for another major core meltdown. Everyone has forgotten the partial meltdown at Three Mile Island and the major catastrophe at Chernobyl. The Russians' mistake will lead to the death of nearly 15,000 people in the Soviet Union and Europe. I'm talking about deaths from leukemia and cancer of the lung, breast, and thyroid. Poor Poland was burned the worst by Chernobyl's fire and radiation fallout. You know they hid other fatal mistakes before Chernobyl. Do I need to remind you of the disaster in Japan in 2011? Will Japan ever recover?"

Harry played his last card. Jimmy's wife made her bid exactly.

Jimmy was again the dummy. "Harry, what's the President going to do with the cookie cutter?"

The term "cookie cutter" was the nickname given to the neutron bomb. President Carter had okayed a limited production of this weapon. But with pressure from anti-nuke forces, Congress had outlawed the weapon just like the banning of bacteriological weapons after World War I. Ronald Reagan reversed the policy, but the U.S. only produced a few and never deployed the weapon. The program was completely scrapped in 1993.

Pressure was now being mounted by the Pentagon to reinstate the weapon into the United States nuclear arsenal, because of stockpiles of lethal liquid nerve gas agent VX in several countries, such as Iran and North Korea.

"I don't know, Jimmy. That's a nasty weapon. This bomb releases a large amount of neutrons, which incapacitate and kill most people and animals within minutes. But the victims suffer violent nausea, diarrhea, and other unpleasant symptoms before they die. Anyone on the periphery of the target area dies a slow death of convulsions. It destroys the cell structure of anyone in its range—and it is especially devastating to the central nervous system."

"No bomb is perfect," Jimmy answered gruffly. "This bomb is precise and clean. It does not destroy buildings or military equipment. Remove the dead people and the buildings and equipment could be used within a short time. Just think of what it would do to the rat and roach population!"

Harry chuckled and nodded his head. "The bomb does destroy a few square miles of property. You know my position. I'm for total nuclear disarmament."

"But Harry, the Chinese exploded a neutron bomb in September, 1988. After the Tiananmen Square massacre, the Chinese government started an aggressive espionage program against the U.S. Not by professional spies, but by visiting Chinese students and scientists who play on their American hosts."

"They are trying to stave off a threat from India," Harry shot back as he slammed a card on the table.

"Sure, so they steal the neutron bomb secrets from the Livermore National Laboratory in California. They developed the bomb from the data stolen from this laboratory, and we sit on our hands with the information locked away from our armed forces. We could have used the cookie cutter to get rid of Iraq's Saddam Hussein when he occupied Kuwait. A few bombs would have killed the Iraqi soldiers without destroying the buildings and oil fields. Then we would not have had to invade Iraq."

"Total disarmament would decrease the probability of war," Harry shot back as he slammed a card on the table.

Jimmy saw that Harry was mad so he dropped the discussion. Harry was a "pinko." There was no chance of changing his mind. The President had surrounded himself with the wrong type of advisors. There were other options.

Harry dealt the cards. Jane Cranford began to sit a little more erect in her chair as she picked up each one of her cards. Betty sensed that Jane was probably getting a fantastic hand. Her only hope was that Harry was distracted enough that they would not get a slam.

Harry passed. Betty passed also. Jane bid two spades and gave Harry a withering look that meant you had better do something. Jimmy passed. Harry bid three clubs. Jane immediately bid four no-trump—wanting to know how many aces Harry had. Harry responded six spades. Betty's worst fears were true; Harry and Jane were going to get a slam and from the looks of her hand they were going to make it. Jane bid seven spades without any hesitation. Harry laid down his hand since Jane had introduced spades and Jane looked pleased. She played promptly and methodically. Betty and Jimmy had no hope of setting them. Jane smiled as she pulled in the last trick and then totaled up the score.

Harry was feeling a lot better now, because when Jane had a bad
night of cards, things at home were on an uneven keel for a while.
He continued his conversation with Jimmy.

"Jimmy, you should forget about defense and clean up your own
house. Senator Benson said the other day on the Senate floor that
the tax code was ready to crumble under its own weight. Too many
loopholes, deductions, and credits. He's suggesting a Simpliform.
He would substitute a four-line calculation for the present obsta-
cle course on Form 1040."

"Benson's off his rocker," Jimmy replied. "Do you want to throw
one-third of the accountants and lawyers on the welfare rolls? Remember what happened with the tax law after the Tax Reform Act
of 1986? Would you like for me to do away with the charitable con-
tribution deduction? I would have every rabbi, priest, and minister in the country marching on Washington. But maybe Washington
needs some religion. Try doing away with the mortgage deduction
on your home."

"I don't know, Jimmy. Benson indicates that the tax paid by
those with incomes of six figures and above averages less than 30%,
in spite of a statutory rate of 35%. He says that sixty billion dollars
were retained by individuals and corporations last year because of
tax subsidies. He would reduce these subsidies—corporate welfare—and at the same time introduce new lower, overall progres-
sive tax rates," Harry said.

"Besides, equity creates complex laws," Harry continued. "A blind
person receives an extra standard deduction because Congress felt
that such a person had a need for this tax subsidy. Why doesn't a
deaf person or a moron get an extra standard deduction? Congress
passed the childcare expense credit to help support little children
while their mothers work. A tax credit reduces over-all tax liability dollar-for-dollar."

"Would you guys stop talking shop?" said Jane in a combative tone.

The rest of the hands were mediocre. Since Jane and Harry's spade
slam everything else was pale in comparison. Betty, at one time,
thought her hand might have some possibilities, but she couldn't get
any adequate response from Jimmy. She didn't know whether it was

because *he* didn't have a good hand or whether he was afraid he might have to play the hand so he didn't want to show any initiative in introducing new suits. At any rate, she figured she had better not take any chances, which was wise, because Jimmy only had six points and that was including distribution. There would have been little hope to make a slam with support like that from your partner.

About 11:30, Jimmy began yawning and nudging Betty under the table. Betty took the hint and suggested they call it a night. They thanked Jane and Harry for a nice evening even though their cards had not been spectacular.

Jimmy told Harry he would probably be seeing him somewhere around the Hill. He was glad to be going home. It had been a long and frustrating day.

* * *

On Monday, IRS Commissioner Jimmy Callaway reported to the House Ways and Means Committee:

"Recently, I have had the opportunity to conduct a series of visits to a number of our facilities, and to speak to large numbers of IRS employees. I am proud of what I saw. Every day, these individuals perform the tough, complicated, and sometimes dangerous job of making the tax system work. They meet taxpayers face to face to provide assistance, to examine returns, and to collect overdue taxes. They investigate potential fraud, so that dishonest citizens are not allowed to pass their share of the tax burden to others.

"It is unfortunate that IRS employees are increasingly becoming the object of taxpayers' frustration with the tax system. But it is tragic that some of this frustration is resulting in violence. The health care law especially sparked death threats to IRS employees. Threats have increased steadily between 2001 and 2008, with more than 1,200 threats and assault cases being investigated."

"In 2010, Joseph Stack published an anti-tax manifesto before he crashed his small aircraft into the building in Austin, Texas that housed an IRS office. Sixty-four percent of the 755 IRS facilities have no security presence, so we spent more than $100 million in 2010 on office security."

Chapter 10

But we need to quit taxing people upon death [Federal estate tax]. No taxation without respiration.

—Steve King

"The best type of income is tax-saved dollars—it's not taxable." Henry Silverman was beginning one of his daylong seminars.

"My definition of a loophole is something someone else is doing to save taxes." As Vladimir Lenin once said, "the way to crush the bourgeoisie is to grind them between the millstones of taxation and inflation." Henry liked to say the long "b" word.

He had fourteen attendees—the typical businessmen and women and wealthy heirs. Each had paid $1,000 to attend. Henry had offered a $200 discount for this particular seminar.

"In a non-academic book entitled *The Call Girl*, the author indicates that the tax structure created the high-priced call girl. Entertainment of clients and customers is a 50% deductible expense under the income tax laws, and a call girl's fee can be treated as a business expense for tax purposes. In effect, the U.S. Treasury frequently pays more than one-half the cost of the entertainment.

"Now gentlemen, if a call girl's fee...."

Henry noticed someone vaguely familiar in the back row. "Wait a minute, that's Burke, the IRS agent," Henry thought. "He has a wig on, but he can't hide his mustache." He poured himself a glass of water and took a swallow in order to stall for time while he decided what to do. How did he get in here?

He must have paid the fee. What can I do? Much of my material is about evasion. If I drop the material, I'm dead. If I recommend fraud and evasion, I can be locked up. Is this like the life of an earthworm during a heavy rainstorm? If the worm stays in the ground, he drowns. If he surfaces, a bird will probably eat him.

Several of the attendees looked around at each other. They were surprised at the long pause in the middle of a sentence.

"Ladies and gentlemen, I'm sorry, but we have an IRS agent in the room. It would be unfair to you if I continued this seminar. So I'm going to refund your money. I'll keep you informed of my next seminar. Rest assured that the agent will not learn your names. Thank you."

Henry walked back to Jeff Burke. "Hello, Mr. Burke, can I help you?"

Jeff was stunned. He thought that Silverman might recognize him with the black wig, but he would never have guessed that he would cancel the seminar. At fourteen times $1,000, he was giving back $14,000.

Jeff noticed that the other thirteen individuals were quickly leaving the room. Jeff had wanted their names. But Silverman was still shaking his hand.

"Er, you didn't have to cancel the seminar. I only wanted to learn the latest tax avoidance techniques." Jeff smiled ruefully.

Controlling his anxiety, Henry responded, "Well, you know how it is. You caught me napping. I don't wish to give away any of my trade secrets. You might retire early and go into competition with me."

By now Jeff was regaining composure. "Mr. Silverman, on Wednesday I will present you with a summons for a list of individuals who have attended your seminars for the past two years. Also, I want a list of the subscribers to your newsletter, 'How to Cheat and Defraud the IRS.'"

"Why Mr. Burke, you know that the courts would not uphold a summons for a fishing expedition."

"We'll see," Jeff responded with a little humor in his eyes. Jeff turned and left the room.

Henry was disappointed. He had added an IBOB evasion scheme to his lecture. Suppose Ms. Jones owns 99 percent of Jones Company and Jones Company owns 99 percent of New Co. New Co owns a hotel worth $2.5 million with a $1 million basis. So if New Co sells the hotel, there will be a $1.5 million capital gain.

Enter the Installment Sale Bogus Optional Basis transaction or IBOB. Ms. Jones sets up a family trust which buys the hotel for $2.5 million, but gives a $2.5 million installment note to New Co. The family trust never pays the installment note, but theoretically has a $2.5 million tax basis in the hotel. So when the family trust sells the hotel to an unrelated party for $2.6 million, there will only be a $100,000 capital gain (rather than a $1.1 million taxable gain). Henry learned of this scheme on the GAO website.

Under his breath, Henry hummed Tom T. Hall's country song: "Faster horses, younger women, older whiskey, and smarter tax advisors." He did not like hip-hop songs.

* * *

Henry was meeting with Carl Strovee and Strovee's lawyer. The meeting with the IRS agent was scheduled for tomorrow. Some kind of strategy had to be developed.

Carl, fidgeting in his chair, had the first question for Ted Abbott, a Harvard lawyer who specialized in taxation. Ted was slim and fortyish, had a receding hairline, and wore round silver-rimmed glasses. "Should we cooperate with the IRS?"

"Well, I have two rules of thumb. Point one, if a taxpayer has a strong position or evidence that demonstrates a weakness in the government's case, cooperate and produce the requested information. Point two, if your position is weak and you cannot punch holes in the agent's case, avoid him. Don't cooperate."

"A good strategy is to offer the agent any information that he can obtain elsewhere. Thus, you look like you are cooperating. For example, salary information, security transactions, purchases of insurance policies, transactions involving real estate, and bank deposits are items which an agent can obtain with some work. Give it to him since he'll find it anyway."

The attorney paused and then continued. "You told me on the phone that the IRS had found a bank account in your mother's name in Valentine, Nebraska. Is that yours?"

"Yes"

"Did you pay taxes on the money?"

Carl looked over at Henry as he replied, "I thought they were tax-saved dollars."

The attorney slowly shook his head. "Even a fruitcake would give a better answer than that. Remember, now, we have an attorney-client relationship. What you tell me here is confidential and will not be revealed to the IRS or the courts. I am on your side, but I need to know the truth."

Carl did not especially appreciate the term *fruitcake,* but he looked straight at his lawyer and said, "I have been putting about 30% of my income into my mother's bank account. Henry encouraged me to do it. He helped me set up two sets of records."

"Okay, you can't get a reward for cooperating when in fact the evidence appears to the investigating agent that a criminal action is involved. Cooperation will not save you from a conviction. People have gone to jail even though they cooperated with the agent and paid all of the proposed deficiency.

"The deficiency is $47,554," continued the lawyer. "How much money do you have in the Valentine account?"

"About $240,000," replied Carl.

The lawyer again shook his head. "I'll need a substantial retainer, say $50,000. Neither of you are to contact the agent from this point on. I will inform the IRS that all future communication will be conducted through me."

"Mr. Silverman, I want you to attend the conference with me tomorrow with the agents. Don't say anything, however, unless I direct you to. You might tell the agent more than is necessary. It's Henry, isn't it?"

Henry nodded yes.

"Henry, I want you to give Carl all records and relevant documents. Give him your accounting working papers dealing with his tax returns."

"Obviously, Carl, you are not to allow any agents to see these records and documents. We will not provide them with net worth

statements. I've seen too many situations where the net worth increase was calculated on the basis of the taxpayer's own books and
records, which were given to the agent during the investigative
process. I will not cooperate my client to jail. Giving agents net
worth statements is like giving your executioner a lethal weapon."

"Even if we hand them your records, they would demand that
you submit to a formal question-and-answer session under oath. We
don't need that."

"Have you received a large inheritance or other non-taxable income such as insurance proceeds or proceeds from a loan?"

"Nope," responded Carl.

"Is the bank account in your mother's name alone?"

"Yes."

"Did you use her exact name and Social Security number? Did
you use an assumed name?"

"I changed an 'e' to an 'r' and used Mary Strover and her real
Social Security number."

"Guess we'll use the old standby, a cash hoard. We can try to
prove that the bank deposits were in fact accumulated by you and
her in years prior to the tax years in question. Have you put monies
in the bank account on a regular basis?"

"No, about once a year. I would keep the stash in my home safe
and take it to Valentine about once or twice a year when I visited
my mother. Mr. Abbott, would you lay it on the line? What is my
exposure? I don't quite understand this distinction between a *civil*
and *criminal* situation."

"Where should I begin?" Ted looked at Henry. "Have you not
told him anything?"

"Nope, I'm not a lawyer."

"That's evident," the attorney replied with intensity in his voice.

He then turned back to Carl. "The IRS has civil, as well as criminal, sanctions for violations of tax laws. These civil sanctions are
assessed in addition to the tax liability. These civil penalties include
a 5% per month penalty for failure to file a return or a timely re-

turn, a 20% negligence penalty for negligence or intentional disregard, and a 75% civil fraud penalty on an underpayment on any portion which is due to fraud. The purpose of this 75% fraud penalty is a remedial civil sanction in order to safeguard and protect the government revenue and to reimburse the government for the heavy expense of investigation and loss resulting from a taxpayer's fraud."

"Criminal sanctions provide punishment for offenses and generally involve imprisonment and fines. A person who willfully attempts in any manner to evade or defeat a tax may be guilty of a felony and upon conviction may be fined not more than $100,000 and/or imprisonment for not more than five years, together with the costs of prosecution."

"Five years!" Carl almost shouted.

"Yes, and both civil and criminal sanctions may be imposed for the same offense. Manhattan federal prosecutors went after Bernard Madoff's brother and sons for criminal tax fraud. The sons were cooperating with the authorities." The attorney paused to allow Carl to appreciate the severity of his situation.

Then the attorney continued in a somber voice. "The burden and measure of proof differs in criminal and civil cases. In a criminal case, the IRS must prove every fact of the offense and show guilt beyond a reasonable doubt. In case of civil fraud, the IRS has the burden of establishing fraud by clear and convincing evidence. You may not be convicted upon mere suspicion or conjecture. Likewise, you should be acquitted if the evidence is equally consistent with innocence as with guilt."

"Now in numerous civil cases,"—the attorney paused and cleared his throat—"the IRS's determination of the deficiency is presumptively correct. The burden is placed upon the taxpayer to overcome this presumption. In other words, the taxpayer is guilty and must prove himself innocent in civil cases."

"What must they do to prove I committed a criminal offense?" Carl asked as he slowly rubbed his hands together.

"Three elements are necessary for a criminal offense. Point one: additional tax due and owing. Point two: an attempt in any manner to evade or defeat any tax. Point three: willfulness—intentional wrong doing."

"As to point one, the IRS must establish that, at the time the offense was committed, an additional tax was due and owing. In essence, you must owe more taxes than you reported. But the IRS does not have to prove evasion of the full amount alleged in the indictment. It is sufficient to show that a substantial amount of the tax was evaded, and this proof need not be measured in terms of gross or net income or by any particular percentage of the tax shown to be due and payable." The attorney talked as if he had given this same discussion many times.

"Apparently, the current policy of the IRS is not to authorize assessment of additional taxes and penalties during the time criminal aspects are pending and to preclude discussion or negotiation looking toward settlement of the civil liability."

"Point two. This phrase 'attempt in any manner' does not mean that one whose efforts are unsuccessful cannot commit the crime of willful attempt. The crime is complete when the attempt is made and nothing is added to its criminality by success or consummation. The real character of an offense lies, not in the failure to file a return or in the filing of a false return, but rather in the attempt to evade any tax. The term 'attempt' implies some affirmative action or the commission of some overt act." His phone rang twice, but the attorney ignored it.

"The Supreme Court has given certain illustrations from which acts or conduct that attempt to evade or defeat any tax may be inferred: keeping a double set of books; making false entries, alterations, invoices, or documents; destruction of books and records; concealment of assets or covering up sources of income; and handling of one's affairs to avoid making the usual records in transactions of that kind. Obviously, Mr. Strovee, you fit this pattern."

"Willfulness is an essential element of proof with respect to most criminal violations investigated by special agents. This word 'willful' generally means an act done with a bad purpose; without justifiable excuse; stubbornly, obstinately, perversely. The Supreme

Court indicates that this word characterizes an act done without grounds for believing it is lawful or conduct marked by careless disregard whether or not one has the right so to act."

"The most laudable motive is no defense where the act committed is a crime in contemplation of law. For example, you may have intentionally understated your income in order to have sufficient funds to support your mother. Although such motive may be admirable, you have specifically intended to evade payment of your income taxes."

"Don't talk to an agent. Don't sign any statements. Remember that, both of you." The attorney turned and looked directly at Henry. "I was involved in a case several years ago in which the court sustained a conviction for tax evasion. It was a close case of willfulness. Even the court indicated that if the taxpayer had not signed a statement, which tied down the element of willfulness, the taxpayer would probably have won. But the admission by the taxpayer tied the pieces together into a neat package of tax evasion."

"Suppose I filed some amended returns and paid the deficiency. Would this stop a civil or fraud charge?" injected Carl.

"No," Ted shot back. "Even a tentative amended return could be considered an admission of guilt with respect to the amount of tax due and fraudulent intent. Before 1953, the IRS had a policy that if a taxpayer voluntarily disclosed before an investigation had begun that he had willfully failed to file a tax return or his filed return was fraudulent, no criminal prosecution would be recommended. The IRS has announced that it will not follow a voluntary disclosure policy."

"In a 1954 court case a taxpayer on the advice of counsel, submitted amended returns clearly marked 'tentative.' The returns showed a substantial increase in the tax payable. The returns were never filed and the taxes were not paid. Yet at the criminal trial, the IRS indicated that by submitting these 'tentative' amended returns, the taxpayer admitted that more taxes were due, and therefore, the evasion was willful. At the subsequent trial, counsel was unable to argue that a lesser deficiency than that indicated on the tentative amended returns was actually due."

"Remember, in order to impose criminal penalties, the IRS must prove you willfully attempted to evade or defeat a tax. They must prove your state of mind." The attorney pointed to his head. "They must prove that your state of mind was evil. That you acted in bad faith and deliberately, not accidentally, tried to evade taxes."

"The Supreme Court indicates that 'willfully,' when used in a criminal context, means an act done with a bad purpose, without justifiable excuse," There was a short pause.

"Henry, you will meet me in front of the IRS building at 12:45 p.m.?" It was more of a demand than a question. Turning to Carl he said, "Now, don't worry. Go home and drink a couple of beers and watch a ball game on the tube. I'll call you tomorrow after the meeting. See you. Oh, before I leave, could you write me that retainer check?"

While Carl was writing the check, the lawyer spoke to Henry. "Did they give Carl his *Miranda* warning when you and he met with the Special Agent?"

"No, but we did not meet with a Special Agent."

The lawyer was referring to the Miranda-type warning which appears in the Special Agent's manual. According to this manual, a *Special* Agent is supposed to properly identify himself and show his credentials. He should also state: "As a Special Agent, one of my functions is to investigate the possibility of criminal violations of the Internal Revenue laws and related offenses." He should give the taxpayer a warning against self-incrimination and explain *his or her* rights to legal counsel.

Carl made a short detour on the way home. He stopped at a travel agency. He purchased a one-way plane ticket to Caracas, Venezuela, under the name J. E. Cajan. Departure time: Wednesday 3:00 p.m.

Carl did not realize that Jeff Burke had already called the Valentine bank. He had slapped a jeopardy assessment against Carl's account. This procedure is used to assess additional taxes and deficiencies when the statutory period for assessment would otherwise expire before the assessment could be made under normal procedures. Jeff had felt that the collection of tax was endangered.

That evening Henry took the tax records involving Carl over to Carl's apartment. Carl seemed to be in reasonable spirits under the circumstances.

Much later that evening, Carl took these tax records along with other personal effects to his self-storage area. He made several trips.

Chapter 11

Nothing is easier than the expenditure of public money. It doesn't appear to belong to anyone. The temptation is overwhelming to bestow it on somebody.

—Calvin Coolidge

Henry Silverman was waiting in front of the IRS building when Ted Abbott arrived. Henry had gotten a haircut earlier. His tight curly black hair was getting too long for his conservative image.

"Hello, Henry, ready for the inquisition?" joked Ted.

"Sure," was the uneasy response.

Minutes later Ted Abbott introduced himself to Jeff Burke and Yvonne Talbert. He informed the two agents that his client, Carl Strovee, would not attend the meeting. He gave them a copy of a power of attorney, Form 2848, signed by Carl.

"My client was unable to get together a net worth statement within such a short period of time," Ted continued. "Aside from the net worth statement, we shall get you a list of bank deposits, his purchases of insurance policies, several transactions in real estate, and his stock brokerage transactions. We do wish to cooperate within limits."

"I'm glad you are going to cooperate, Mr. Abbott," Jeff said "That's really the best way. But you realize that a taxpayer has ten days to answer our summons."

"Mr. Silverman, did you bring in your working papers and other records regarding Mr. Strovee?" asked Jeff.

"Actually, Mr. Strovee has all applicable working papers and documents with respect to his tax returns. I basically used data that was furnished to me by Carl. Any documents that I used were returned to Carl's office after I finished with them."

"Mr. Silverman, you signed the minutes of Mr. Strovee's corporation involving the Section 1244 stock. Did you prepare these minutes?"

"Yes, I did," responded Henry.

"Were the minutes prepared contemporaneously?"

"Sure."

"We have prepared a short statement which indicates that you prepared the minutes and you believe them to be valid. Would you read this and sign it?"

Jeff handed the statement to Henry.

Henry read it and then gave it to Ted. Ted read it.

"Looks okay to me, Henry," said Ted as he handed the statement back to Henry.

Jeff handed a pen to Henry. "Would you sign the statement?"

"No," said Henry.

Jeff did not seem surprised. Next he gave an envelope to Henry. "Here is an administrative summons directing you to produce copies of all tax returns prepared by you for the past three years. If you do not have copies of any returns, please provide us with the names, addresses, and social security numbers of these taxpayers. Also, we want a list of the names and addresses of the subscribers to your newspaper."

Ted watched dumbfounded. The agent did not seem to be going after Carl Strovee. They were after Henry. He was being cunningly outmaneuvered. Ted knew that Jeff had just given Henry an open-ended John Doe summons. Although some courts have held that these types of summonses are invalid, the general rule is that John Doe summonses are enforceable and not unreasonable within the Fourth Amendment.

The John Doe summonses were used frequently in the 70's to uncover incompetent and unscrupulous tax preparers. An agent would submit a standard set of facts to a suspected tax preparer and request that a return be prepared. If the prepared tax return was incorrect, the IRS would issue a summons to the preparer for the names, addresses, and social security numbers of the people for whom he had prepared a return.

Recently, the IRS used a John Doe Summons against UBS. Eventually UBS paid a $780 million fine, delivered 280 names of serious U.S. tax evaders, and basically traded a century of Swiss banking secrecy in order to survive.

Ted also recognized that this was a so-called "chain" investigation. The examination of one taxpayer leads to a fraud investigation of another taxpayer having a relationship with the first. For example, while examining one business, an agent may notice that checks payable to a customer were cashed rather than deposited in the payee's bank account or were endorsed over to a third party. A collateral examination may be undertaken on the customer.

Ted noticed that Jeff was again addressing Henry.

"Mr. Silverman, you are in a lot of trouble. I believe it is fair to tell you that we know that the minutes were backdated. The Treasury Department has a program called ink tagging. Most ink manufacturers change their chemical formulations each year. Each change represents a date prior to which that particular ink did not exist."

"We had the minutes analyzed by our scientists at the Bureau of Alcohol, Tobacco and Firearms. The ink on the minutes was compared with the standard ink samples kept in the library. Your ink matches a library ink that did not exist when the document was dated."

Henry sat in his seat with a defeated look on his face.

Ted had heard of ink sleuths before. Apparently ink tagging aided the prosecutors in the case against former Vice-President Spiro Agnew. An individual had kept a diary of the kickbacks given to Agnew. Scientists were able to verify that all the inks used were available at the time of the entries. Further, the sequence of the entries showed a random pattern consistent with day-to-day work in a diary. Needless to say, in 1973 Agnew pleaded no contest to income tax evasion.

In another court decision, a Texas businessman withdrew $15,000 from his company. He claimed that the money was a loan and therefore tax-free. The IRS said the sum was a taxable dividend. The Texan had to prove that he intended to repay the money at the time of the transfer. He produced a promissory note which he claimed to have signed in December of the year he received the money. Two ink experts testified that the ink used to sign the note was not manufactured until a year and a half later. The Texan met his Alamo.

Jeff was not finished with Henry. "Mr. Silverman, we do want the working papers and other records involving Mr. Strovee's tax returns. I hope you are familiar with the facts in the *Couch* decision? I suggest you also peruse the case of *U.S. v. Edmond.*"

Both Henry and Ted were familiar with the *Couch* decision. Here a summons had been served upon an accountant to obtain his working papers with respect to a client. The accountant ignored the summons and surrendered the records to an attorney. The purpose of this transfer was to allow the taxpayer to use his Fifth Amendment right to keep the working papers away from the IRS.

The Supreme Court held that constitutional rights cannot be enlarged by such a transfer. The rights and obligations of the parties became fixed when the summons was served. A transfer of the records can *not* alter these rights and obligations. The attorney had to give the working papers to the IRS.

Henry had never heard of *Edmond.* He merely nodded yes.

Ted realized that he was losing control of the interview. "Excuse me, Mr. Burke, I'm sure you are aware that any evidence obtained by misrepresentation and deception will not be allowed in a court of law."

"What do you mean by deception?"

"You failed to give my client, Carl Strovee, the proper *Miranda* warning when you interviewed him with Mr. Silverman. You used trickery and deceit in order to obtain evidence—the minutes— from my client. You did not tell him he had the right to refuse to answer questions, and that he could obtain legal counsel. Furthermore, today you failed to give these same warnings to Mr. Silverman."

"Yvonne interviewed Carl Strovee not me. She is not a Special Agent." Jeff turned and spoke to Henry. "Mr. Silverman, did you read my credentials when I handed them to you earlier? Did you know that I was a Special Agent?"

"Uh, yes," Henry replied.

Jeff turned to Ted Abbott. "You know that the manual rules are for internal administration and are not constitutionally mandated. Courts have refused to make the *Miranda* warnings fundamental to due process."

"Correction," Ted shot back, "*some* courts have refused to make them fundamental to due process. This whole charade has been a sneaky, deliberate deception to obtain the minutes of the corporation."

"Surely, Mr. Abbott, you remember the *Prudden* decision. The mere failure of an agent to warn a taxpayer that an investigation may result in criminal charges, assuming they are not acts by the agent which materially misrepresent the nature of inquiry, does not constitute fraud, deceit, or trickery. Do you want me to give you a citation to this case?"

"No, but I have a copy of the *Tweel* decision for you to read. I've underlined some passages pertinent to this situation." The attorney handed Jeff several pages.

Jeff was worried. He should have given the *Miranda* warning verbally. How could he have forgotten? He knew that although investigative subterfuge has long been an indispensable tool of tax law enforcement, since *Tweel*, any introduction of an agent must include his actual title. Jeff knew that the lawyer was correct. Some courts had held that the failure to give the *Miranda* warning would require suppression of any evidence received. But there had been some erosion of this doctrine during the Reagan era.

The lawyer interrupted Jeff's thoughts. "You are, of course, aware of the exclusion rule. Any evidence obtained illegally by the IRS cannot be used against a taxpayer in any criminal proceeding. The minutes are inadmissible evidence because they were obtained from my client without prescribed warnings or assistance of counsel."

"You are entitled to your opinion, Mr. Abbott, but you are wrong."

"We shall see." The lawyer stood up and said, "Mr. Silverman, I believe it is time for us to leave."

As both Ted and Henry were leaving, Jeff looked directly at Henry and said, "You'll have the materials, which we want by next Wednesday, I hope."

"Yeah," Henry replied softly.

Ted was mad as they walked out of the IRS building. "Why didn't you tell me that you had backdated the minutes of that meeting?" he angrily demanded.

Henry shot back, "How did I know those federal snoopers had an ink tagging program? Nothing is sacred anymore. Pretty soon they'll be checking our urine on a weekly basis to determine our weekly expenditures."

"You should know better than to backdate records," the lawyer responded to the outburst.

"What court do you suggest we go to?"

"Well, you should know the rule of thumb. If you have the law in your favor, go to the U.S. Tax Court; if you have the facts in your favor, go to the district court; and if you have neither in your favor, you go to the U.S. Court of Federal Claims."

Henry just shook his head.

"Well, we've got two turkeys in the frying pan now. I hope you realize that anyone who willfully aids or assists in, counsels or advises the preparation of a document, which is false or fraudulent as to any material matter, is guilty of a felony. I suggest you read Section 7206 of the Internal Revenue Code. Then you may wish to give me a call. I'll need a more substantial retainer—say $15,000 more."

Under his breath, Henry mumbled, "Forget it." Henry went back to his office and looked up Section 7206(5)(B). He was guilty of a felony. Upon conviction he could be fined not more than $100,000, or imprisoned not more than three years, or both, together with the costs of prosecution.

Next Henry found *U.S. v. Edmond.* More bad news. Here a public accountant, who was basically a return-preparer, gave his working papers to his taxpayer-client after receipt of an IRS summons. In court the taxpayer maintained that the working papers were stolen from his automobile, where they were stored. The accountant was found guilty of civil contempt and assessed compensatory damages of $4,000. He avoided a jail sentence only because it was possible for him to purge himself of the contempt citation by delivering the "stolen" records to the IRS.

Henry checked some material dealing with John Doe summons. These are third-party summonses that do not name the person with respect to whose liability they are issued. He found that such a summons may be issued only after an ex parte court proceeding in which the IRS establishes that:

1) the summons relates to the investigation of a particular person or ascertainable group or class of persons,

2) there is a reasonable basis for believing that such person, group, or class of persons may have failed to pay income taxes, and

3) the information sought to be obtained from the examination of the records was not readily available from other sources.

So the agents were bluffing here. They would have to bring a lawsuit to get this information.

Henry was nervous when he dialed Carl Strovee's phone number. He couldn't afford a conflict with the IRS. A messy conflict would adversely affect his tax practice, especially his seminars. Who would attend a seminar taught by someone who got caught?

There was no answer. Carl was normally at home.

After trying Carl's number for about two hours, Henry went over to Carl's apartment. No one answered the doorbell.

Henry told the doorman that he was afraid that Carl had had a heart attack.

When the doorman opened Carl's door, Henry was stunned. The apartment was stripped of any of Carl's personal effects. All of his paintings were gone. The safe was open. Henry knew that Carl had left—for good.

For $50, the doorman allowed Henry to look around the apartment. Henry could not find his working papers. He was as good as dead.

Chapter 12

Your federal government needs your money so that it can perform vital services for you that you would not think up yourself in a million years.

—Dave Barry

Last night had been successful for Jeff Burke. His surveillance of the Flesher garbage dumpster had finally paid off. He found one dollar, four aluminum cans, *and* the practice run of the football slips used in the gambling racket in Baltimore. They had printed the slips for the next two weeks and had forgotten to destroy the discarded slips.

Jeff was jubilant when he returned to call Hank Brown, the other Special Agent helping with the Flesher case. Actually, it was Hank's "jacketed case." Jeff helped Hank out with the surveillance.

"Hello, Hank; got some good news. Flesher ran off the football slips yesterday, and I found the practice run. I have them in an envelope on my desk. Should I send it to the FBI and get the fingerprints lifted?"

"Great! Yes, send them in. Let them know that *your* prints are on it. I don't want them to lock you up. This case may have more significance than we thought. Guess who is the owner of the plumbing outlet? Ms. Andre Flesher, the wife of B.W. Flesher. She works there three or four hours, several times a week, but draws a $72,000 salary. Probably unreasonable compensation."

"Super! We'll disallow part of her salary. I better check on the pen register. I'll get that off before we blow the case."

"You're right. Get that off fast!"

"I'll call my man and get him to take it off tonight. What do we do now?"

"I'm going to watch the plumbing shop this afternoon and to-morrow. I'll photograph anyone who enters or leaves the place. I believe their gambling operation is in the back. I've been inside — bought some washers for my leaking spigots. Would you believe I fixed two last night? Maybe I could disguise myself as a plumber and infiltrate the organization."

"You could probably make more money. A plumber is paid well. But you'll have to join a union," joked Jeff.

Hank likes to joke himself but resented anyone else who fol-lowed through with a joke. "Anyway," he broke in, "there is a door which leads to the back room. The front room seems small com-pared to the length of the building. We probably should begin to make plans for raiding the plumbing shop. Should we raid the porno shop and the printing shop also?"

"I don't know," replied Jeff. "Let me think about it awhile. I'll call you tomorrow and let you know the results of the pen register."

After hanging up, Jeff called his telephone man and instructed him to remove the pen register at the plumbing outlet. Jeff asked his contact to call him back in the morning and let him know the number of outgoing calls.

Jeff took the discarded football cards and wrote his initials and date on the back of them with his anthracene pencil. He did this so that he could later testify that they were the cards he found. Anthracene is a substance that can be obtained either in powder form or pencil form. It is invisible, but gives off a brilliant fluo-rescence when exposed to ultraviolet light. It can be placed on documents or other objects that a Special Agent might want to identify later.

He then made a copy of the cards and put them in a large, brown envelope, writing a description of the contents on the face of the envelope. He then sent the envelope to the FBI fingerprinting division.

Jeff began jotting down some notes. He drew a diagram of B.W. Flesher's known business associates.

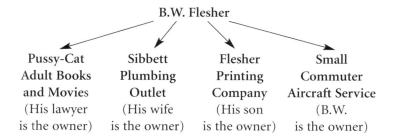

The businesses were called brother-sister corporations in tax jargon. B.W. Flesher had all the trademarks of an organized crime member. Or he was a front for someone else. The plumbing outlet was owned by his wife; it was probably a front for gambling.

His fourteen-year-old son was the owner of the printing company. It was an S corporation. It was probably a legitimate business, except that it probably printed the pornographic books. Nothing wrong with a minor child owning an S corporation. Good tax planning, thought Jeff. An S corporation is taxed like a partnership—no double taxation, yet it gives limited liability to the shareholders.

Flesher's lawyer was apparently the "front" or "nominee" owner of the pornographic business. Well-known criminals or underworld figures often place their business operations in the name of their lawyer to lend an aura of respectability to the business. Trusted girlfriends or wives have been known to hide assets for racketeers.

Retail adult bookstores are generally not directly owned by members of organized crime. Although the porno business itself is legal, investigative experience indicates that large amounts of income are never reported for tax purposes.

The video/bookstore is one of the largest and most profitable outlet of pornography. Here sex-oriented books, magazines, photography, "peep shows," films, and other erotic items are displayed and sold. Illegal hardcore pornography material is often sold "under the counter" for regular customers who are not suspected of being the police.

Sexually oriented manuscripts are purchased from individuals at nominal prices. These manuscripts are then sent to a printing establishment for volume printing and the books are later sold to related or controlled corporations. These corporations may be shell corporations to provide legal insulation. The books are then distributed to local retail stores to be sold to the general public. The printing company may never receive payment for the books.

The small commuter aircraft company might be involved in narcotics. The planes may be used to smuggle drugs into the country. The narcotics business is organized like a legitimate importing-wholesaling-retailing business. Only organized crime could provide the large amount of funds and the international connections necessary for a long-term cocaine distribution system.

Then again, Jeff thought, the aircraft business might be legitimate. A prominent figure in organized crime may not have a legitimate source of funds. Often his only means of support is from income realized through illegal activities. Thus, in order to be able to prove how he supports himself and his family, the individual has to have a source of legal income, which he reports for income tax purposes. He must find a business, which will put him on the payroll and issue him a regular payroll check. Sometimes these payroll payments are returned to the business in cash and diverted.

Flesher's wife was receiving a large salary for the performance of few services for the plumbing company. Mr. Flesher may be getting a large salary from the aircraft company, Jeff hypothesized.

A stab of doubt erupted inside Jeff. Maybe he and Hank were all wrong. Maybe all these businesses were legitimate. Maybe the businesses were operating labor black markets.

During the Carter administration, a combination of high inflation and tax increases imposed a heavy tax burden on individual businesses. Labor unions continued to increase in power, and United States goods became too high priced to compete with foreign goods.

But Ayn Rand, author and conservative philosopher, had been wrong. In her classic book, *Atlas Shrugged*, her heroes, producers and workers, just stopped working because of the oppressive gov-

ernmental regulations and high income taxes. When all the producers went on strike, the world collapsed.

Rather than really striking, the U.S. taxpayers went underground.
Many Americans adopted the Latin approach to the problem of the
disappearing value of the dollar. A network of unofficial jobs was
created in a secret economy. This clandestine industry became
known as the labor black market.

More than 10 million individuals worked part time or full time
at jobs that did not officially exist. Entire families worked at home
in the basement or in a hidden room making towels, shoes, furni-
ture, and other necessities. Barbers worked after hours doing electrical or plumbing chores. Policemen worked after hours as
carpenters. There were rumors that some Southern states were tac-
itly encouraging the labor black market.

Why? Wages at these unofficial jobs were substandard. But with
no tax or social security payments, these low salaries might be
higher than the counterpart salary with federal and state tax rates
as high as 45%. Even ministers were not paying social security taxes
on the fair rental value of the houses provided by their churches.

Pro-union laws do not allow employers to fire inefficient or un-
needed employees. Soaring fringe benefit payments and high official wages resulted in runaway inflation. Right-to-work laws were
outlawed. The government merely ignored the continued deterio-
ration in the U.S. balance of trade.

Americans adopted the sport of fiddling. This game of fiddling
is slang for cheating; tax evasion became popular. The short-lived
reduction in individual tax rates in 2003 did not stop fiddling.
Plumbers, carpenters, and other home-repair specialists began to
quote two prices for a repair job; one price for payment by check
and a lower price for a cash payment. The cash payment could easily be shielded from the tax collector. Even salaried employees began
to pad their expense accounts, often with the tacit approval of their
employers. This mechanism allowed the employees to receive tax-
free income. The high tax burden and the price increases out-
stripping the wage increases were the prime causes of the new nation
of fiddlers.

Part of the United States' problem had been the slow growth in productivity and output since the early 1960s. Even poor Great Britain had experienced more per capita growth than the United States. The low 2% increase in real output per employed individual had been due to resources being applied to government and consumption and not enough resources devoted to United States capital formation. Capital formation is what makes growth possible.

Some economists believe that the multiple taxation of income, which is saved and invested, has caused a fundamental bias against capital formation. Income that is saved is taxed at higher rates than income used for consumption. Why? Income spent on consumer goods is taxed only once, whereas a second tax must be paid on dividends, interest, and gains that result from investing or saving income. Quite naturally, United States individuals save and invest less. The elimination of the favorable capital gain rates during the Reagan administration only compounded the problem. At least favorable capital gain rates for individuals came back in the mid-nineties. Still, about 97 percent of the federal income tax is paid by 50 percent of the taxpayers. Poor people do not pay taxes, and the tax base must be expanded—not made smaller.

Maybe, Jeff thought, we'll find out if Flesher is a crook when we raid his places.

Chapter 13

Where there is an income tax, the just man will pay more
and the unjust less on the same amount of income.

—Plato

Jeff noticed the short item in the paper himself.

Two Baltimore police officials found $77,240 in the back
of a van stopped for a drunk driving arrest and took the
funds into custody for 'safekeeping.'
According to the local press, the van was driven by Charles
Z. Samson, and the money in $50 and $100 bills was
banded into $1,000 stacks and stuffed in brown paper bags
under the vehicle's back seat.
Samson denied knowledge of the money and told officers
the van belonged to the company for whom he worked.

Jeff called the police department and learned that the van was
owned by Sibbett Plumbing Outlet. What a break! Probably the
money was being transferred in Flesher's gambling racket.

Jeff called Hank Brown and gave him the details. Hank prepared
a quick assessment and seized the money. Since Charles Samson
had previously been arrested for allegedly smuggling marijuana
and cocaine, Hank seized his home, his Chevrolet pickup, and his
bank account. To rub it in, Hank placed a lien on the $5,000 bond
that an anonymous friend posted for his release from police custody.

In addition to seizures for tax purposes, the IRS can seize assets
related to the sale or transfer of illegal narcotics. These seizures include items used to transport (e.g., vehicles, planes, boats, ranches,
houses, and businesses). It is through these seizures that the IRS
gets a lot of cars for special agents to drive.

Hank informed Mr. Samson that he owed $87,500 in taxes, payable immediately, on income earned to that point. Hank told Jeff that he wanted to be tough on Mr. Samson in the hopes that he would confess that he was a pick-up man for Mr. Flesher.

It was not uncommon for seizures and assessments to sometimes far exceed apparent tax liability. The Nixon administration, before Watergate, had used effectively the little-known tax law that provides for quick assessment, called jeopardy assessment, and seizure of taxes from people who appear to be about to flee in a crusade against illicit drug dealers.

Operating in ninety metropolitan areas and over a two-and-a-half-year period, over $27 million was seized by the IRS and an additional $101 million was assessed against 3,500 drug suspects.

The seizure law is more than a half-century old. The law is vague and places few restrictions upon the IRS. The language of the law leaves the courts with little cause for intervention.

Local police departments often work closely with IRS agents. If the police arrest someone and the person has a sizable amount of money, the arresting officer may immediately call the IRS. Where there are indications that the person is dealing in drugs, gambling, or other illegal activities, the agent will make a large tax assessment and grab the individual's money or property to cover the assessment. The agent may seize the assets even before making the formal assessment.

Jeff recalled one episode that occurred while he was working in the Miami office. Apparently Sharon Mills, a former National Airlines stewardess, was arrested for speeding in northern Miami. Rather than writing a speeding ticket, the plainclothesmen took her to the police station. Instead of being policemen, they were actually narcotics agents, and they searched her purse. They found $4,420 in cash, a small bottle containing four pills, and a .38 Colt revolver.

She was charged with speeding, carrying a concealed weapon, and possession of drugs. The IRS seized her money, several rings, and other jewelry she was wearing. The IRS informed Ms. Mills that she owed $25,449 in back taxes and seized her safe deposit box at her bank.

Apparently Ms. Mills, a divorcee, lived with George Craver, who was alleged in court to be a major seller and smuggler of marijuana and cocaine. Craver had never been charged with these crimes and denied dealing drugs.

In court, an IRS agent indicated that the $25,449 tax assessment was the tax on an estimated commission Ms. Mills allegedly received for helping Craver and others sell cocaine. In further testimony, the agent admitted that neither the police nor the IRS had any evidence that Ms. Mills participated in the scheme or derived any income from it. They could only prove that Ms. Mills lived with George Craver.

The police charges were dropped against Ms. Mills. She was found innocent of speeding. The pills in her purse were prescribed by a doctor, and she carried the gun legally. There was no known evidence that the $4,420 came from an illicit source.

When Jeff left Miami, the IRS still had the money, the safe deposit box, and the $25,449 assessment was in effect. Reason: Assessment and collection of tax may be restrained by the courts only when 1) it was clear that under no circumstances could the IRS ultimately prevail, *and* 2) the taxpayer would suffer irreparable injury for which there is no adequate remedy under law.

Hank called Jeff later in the afternoon. "Jeff, we are going to raid the plumbing and printing shop tomorrow morning."

Jeff asked, "Do we have probable cause?" Jeff knew that a warrant must be based upon probable cause to be valid. This elusive concept of probable cause consists of facts or circumstances, which would lead a reasonably cautious and prudent person to believe that:

1) the person to be arrested is committing a crime or has committed a felony, or
2) the property subject to seizure is on the premises to be searched and an offense involving it has been or is being committed.

"The fact that a large sum of money was found in the plumbing truck and the discarded practice run of the gambling tickets in the outside garbage bin should be enough evidence for probable cause," Hank reasoned.

But Jeff asked, "Was the garbage bin evidence obtained in violation of constitutional provisions and therefore not permissible in a later trial?"

"No, the evidence from the garbage bin is okay," answered Hank. "When an individual throws records in a trash can, the person has abandoned the records and cannot claim that you violated his rights under the Fourth Amendment."

"You're probably right," agreed Jeff.

"We will meet at 8:00 in the morning for instructions. There will be eight of us in the search party."

"I'll be there with bells on my toes."

At eight o'clock, Hank addressed the seven assembled people. Hank was the raid leader. He had organized the search party, and he was charged with the responsibility of conducting the search.

"Good morning. I decided to raid Flesher before they move their operations. With the police finding the $77,000 in the plumbing truck and us slapping liens on the truck and the money, they may decide to move out. I believe they are operating a gambling racket in the plumbing outlet. Also, I believe they store wagering paraphernalia in both the plumbing and printing shop."

"Here is a copy of the search warrant. The warrant is based upon information, that I provided Magistrate Howard yesterday. He reviewed my affidavit, placed me under oath, and I signed the affidavit. He issued the warrant, which is good for ten days. But I wish to hit as soon as possible."

"The remainder of the raid kit you have contains the normal items. Let me review them since this is the first raid for Jane Henderson. Good luck, Jane." Hank motioned to a smiling Jane sitting on his right.

"There's an arrest warrant. Please take a couple of minutes to read my memo setting forth the plan for the raid, responsibilities of each of you, and a description of the suspected violators. There is a detailed map showing the location and approximate interior layout of both the plumbing and printing shops. You have masking tape to seal entry and discharge chambers of any gaming devices.

Also, money wrappers, pencils, writing pads, paper sacks, and a hand stapler are included.

"You have the following forms:

Seized property notice and identification tags;
Inventory record of seized vessels, vehicles, and aircrafts;
Special monies reports;
Appraisement list for seized personal property;
Seized property report;
Affidavits; and
Summons."

Jeff quickly read through the memo explaining the plan of the raid. He noticed that he would go with Hank, Jane, the greenhorn, and a fourth agent to the plumbing outlet. He and Hank would enter the front door. Jane and the other agent would cover the back exit. They were to use subterfuge to gain entrance to the backroom.

"Are there any questions?" Hank was speaking again. Seeing that there were no questions, Hank continued. "We have secured mobile phones. We will try to enter both places at the same time. I will call you. When I give the signal 'cantaloupe,' go to your designated entry point and enter."

Jeff and the three agents parked near the plumbing outlet at 9:45. Hank said, "Okay, let's set our watches. I have 9:45. Frank, you and Jane go to the corner. When you see us get out, go directly to the back door. Do not try to enter until exactly 10:00."

At 9:57, Jeff called the other mobile unit and gave the speaker to Hank. At 9:59, Hank spoke firmly the word "cantaloupe" twice into the speaker. "Did you copy?"

"10-4" was the response.

Jeff and Hank walked briskly toward the plumbing outlet. Once inside the business Hank walked up to the counter, and showed his credentials. As Jeff walked behind the counter to the door leading to the back room, he saw the employee's hand reach under the counter and push a button.

Hank identified himself and began to read the search warrant to the employee.

The door was locked. Jeff knocked on the door. "We are fed-eral agents with a search warrant. Open up immediately!" he shouted.

Jeff waited a reasonable amount of time—about three seconds. He knocked again. "Open the door. I'm a federal agent with a search warrant," Jeff roared. No one answered, but he could hear what sounded like paper shredders.

After several more seconds Jeff stepped back and then smashed his shoulder into the door; it didn't open. He hit it again; his shoulder was hurting. The door didn't open. He then stuck a crowbar near the lock of the door and firmly yanked on it. There was a sharp, cracking sound. Jeff crashed into the door again. It flew open.

Jeff shouted, "Come on, Frank!" Jeff saw several employees shov-ing reports and paper into two shredding machines. Still other peo-ple were throwing papers into a fire and washing papers in a sink.

Hank came in behind Jeff, pushing the outside employee on the floor. He shouted, "Stop that, you are under arrest. There's a fed-eral law against the destruction of evidence." Flash paper is used by both magicians and numbers' operators.

Frank and the other agent could not get in the back door. Jeff ran to the back door and unlocked it. When he turned around he saw that the employees were still shredding and burning evidence.

Jeff ran toward the front since Hank was heading for the shred-ders. With his gun still drawn, Jeff shoved two people away from the fire. The paper shredders became silent as Hank pulled the plugs.

The greenhorn agent turned off the water. Apparently, the records were water-soluble rice paper. Jeff noticed one employee putting his hand inside a drawer at his desk. Jeff turned and pointed his gun directly at the baldhead of the man and said firmly, "With-draw that hand very slowly, or you are a dead man."

The man was so surprised and frightened that he actually fell back-ward in his chair. Jeff moved to the desk drawer expecting to see a pistol. Instead he saw a buzzer inside the desk drawer. Jeff turned toward the man on the floor and asked, "What's the buzzer for?"

The man merely shook his head. Jeff walked over and raised his gun as if to strike the man. The man covered his head with his arms and began shouting, "Don't hit me! Please don't hit me!"

Jeff didn't. He knew that a Special Agent can use only that degree of force necessary to ensure compliance with the order of arrest. Use of excessive force could subject him to lawsuits and disciplinary action. A gun may be drawn from a holster only if an agent's life or that of a fellow law enforcement officer is in danger.

But the man would not tell him what was the purpose of the buzzer.

They had hit the jackpot, however. There was a row of about twenty telephones used in the bookmaking racket. The employees were unable to destroy all of the papers and records, which could be used in a later trial. About one-half of the large room was filled with coin-operated gaming devices and other gambling paraphernalia.

Two agents took all of the employees to the front of the room and began the process of fingerprinting all of them. Each individual was advised of his or her constitutional rights. Ms. Andre Flesher was not working, but Rob's old lady was among the employees caught. "Too bad," thought Jeff, "Rob may have to go to work."

Jeff and Hank began the tedious search of the entire establishment. All articles that could be of evidentiary value were marked with anthracene pencils for identification. The markings did not injure the evidence itself, yet were not subject to obliteration. The markings denoted which agent found the item, the date, time, and exact spot where it was located. They made photographs of the back room and the paraphernalia and the property. Photographs would make it easier to refresh their memories at the time of the trial.

Once the tagging was complete, they brought the person who they thought was in charge of the operation into the back room. They made an inventory of all the property they were going to seize in the presence of the man. Hank had the man sign a copy of the warrant and a signed copy of the inventory of the seized property.

They closed down the plumbing outlet. They padlocked the doors. They placed the following sign with bright red letters on both the front and back doors: "WARNING: United States Government Seizure." They seized the four plumbing trucks in the back lot.

It had been a good day. Enough records were found to estimate the volume of bookmaking activity that had occurred for the past several years. The seized betting slips and other documents would be excellent evidence to impose the wagering excise tax against the owner.

As expected, there were only three days of records. Records are destroyed after three days. But they would be able to determine the gross volume per day. If they could place Flesher in business for three years, they would be able to extrapolate backwards to calculate the 2% excise tax on the illegal gross daily receipts.

There is, of course, a wagering excise tax on the "take" of anyone in the business of accepting wagers. Then, of course, there were the corporate income taxes owed on the income from the entire operation.

They would be able to project the average daily receipts from the seized records over the time Flesher had been in operation. Jeff knew that courts will generally accept such projections by the IRS unless the taxpayer can prove otherwise. As one court indicated, it is immaterial whether the IRS proceeded upon the wrong theory in determining the deficiency. The taxpayer has the burden of showing that the assessment is wrong upon proper theory.

The other four agents found some gambling paraphernalia, pornographic books, and movies at the printing shop. Hank joked that the agents would have a good time sorting through the seized materials making sure it was pornographic. "How else can a determination be made that the books and movies are 'porno' except by reviewing a fair sample of the material?"

Hank indicated that he would begin a surveillance of the Pussycat bookstore and the commuter aircraft service. "When I have probable cause for a raid, I'll be in touch."

Chapter 14

There's nothing that says a man has to take a toll bridge
across a river when there's a free bridge nearby [Referring
to tax avoidance].

—Senator Pat Harrison

Henry Silverman had called Jeff the previous evening. Henry
was obviously scared. He asked Jeff for immunity. Henry was willing to testify against Carl Strovee. But Henry made the mistake of
telling Jeff that Carl had left town.

At first, Jeff would not bite. Suddenly Henry said, "I have some
information about an employee of the IRS. For immunity, I'll give
you the full details of this individual's illegal activities."

Jeff became more cooperative. "I'll give you a tentative promise
of immunity if the IRS employee is significant and you can provide convincing evidence of wrongdoing."

"Look, Jeff, the information is quite valuable." Of course, Jeff
knew that an agent had no authority to make a personal promise
of immunity. Even if the promise is made, it would not be binding on the IRS. Someone higher up in the organization must provide the binding commitment.

"Okay, Henry, I will come down to the jail this afternoon and
talk about it."

In the next morning's paper, a short article appeared:

Henry Silverman, author of a newsletter entitled "How to
Cheat and Defraud the IRS," was held on a $120,000 bond
Tuesday after his arrest on an indictment alleging a violation of federal income tax laws. Silverman, who writes
under the pen name I.M. Clever, was indicted and ar-

rested by IRS intelligence division agents. Silverman appeared before U.S. Magistrate Blane and was charged with knowingly preparing false corporate minutes in connection with a corporate tax matter.

Jeff talked to Henry around 4:30 at the county jail. Henry's information was valuable. He knew Richard Onner.

"Richard Onner attended one of my seminars under an assumed name. He seemed to be interested in how to embezzle money with the use of a computer," Henry related his information to Jeff.

"After the seminar, he took me to dinner. He indicated that he worked for a large company, which received a large amount of cash through the mail. I referred him to an article that appeared in the *Journal of Accountancy* about computer frauds. I figured he was lying about his employer."

"Several weeks went by and he called me again. At least he had his secretary call me. She gave me his name and city. We had lunch. He wanted my advice about how to set up a system whereby a claims reviewer could prepare false claims payable to friends. He wanted the computer to pay the claims automatically."

"He paid me $300 for my time," Henry continued. "Several days later I called his home number in Martinsburg. His girlfriend answered the phone. She gave me his office number. A simple call to his office phone gave me his employer—the IRS. I figure he's ripping off some bread. I'm willing to testify about my meetings with him if you'll get me off the hook. How about it?"

"I can't promise anything, Henry, but I'll try to help you. Keep cool."

When Jeff returned to his office he received an exciting but frightening telephone call. He was not prepared for the call. Detective Garrison was on the other end.

"You found her," the voice almost shouted.

"Found whom?" asked a puzzled Jeff.

"You found the killer. The hair, which you gave me, belonged to the killer. Who is she?"

Jeff was silent for a moment. Why had she not tried to kill him? Maybe she was merely after Nick. But why would she take such a chance and pick him up for a one-night stand?

"Hello! Are you still there?" the voice on the other end of the line broke his concentration. "Who is she?"

"Uh, Deidre Moore," Jeff replied.

Garrison continued, "We used an Aggie nuclear hair analysis. Do you know what an Aggie is? That's an alumnus of Texas A&M University. There must be a thousand Aggie jokes. Did you hear the one about the Aggie who invented an upward ejection seat for a helicopter? That's the joke."

"Anyway, at A&M there's a nuclear hair analyzer. This device analyzes 30 or more characteristics in each strand of hair from a human. A conventional microscope can provide on an average only seven identifiable characteristics such as color and texture. In fact, hair tests are preferable to urinalysis for detecting drug use. A hair will show the degree to which a person is a chemical abuser.

"Neutron activation analysis makes many elements in the hair radioactive. Each element that is irradiated produces a distinct signal, which can be monitored and recorded. A strand of hair is almost as good as a fingerprint. The chance of reproduction of the same combination in another person's hair is one in six million. This number is called the likelihood ratio that the hair on the model airplane matches the hair which you gave me."

Garrison took a deep breath and continued, "There was, of course, surface contamination from the explosion. So both hairs were washed and analyzed. The great thing about forensic activation is that the wash solution can be retained and studied separately from the clean hair. This technique does not destroy the item analyzed. The two hairs can be preserved for use in the courtroom or for further tests."

Garrison chuckled. "My Aggie scientist indicates that some tests showed that Napoleon had ingested a significant amount of arsenic twice during his life, but not enough to kill him. He indicates that the trace elements are significantly different between male and fe-male hair. This difference allows identification of the sex of the supplier of unknown hair at least 90% of the time."

"The murderer of your friend was a woman. The hair, which you gave me, is quite similar to the hair found on the plane. In all likelihood they are the same person. She's a strawberry blonde who uses a rinse to hide the gray hairs. She's in her forties. She has lived around steel mills—maybe she's around Pittsburgh or Gary, Indiana. Good diet, so she is middle or upper class."

"Where can we find her? Where does she live?" the detective asked abruptly.

"I don't know. Wait a minute. Her registration form indicated that she was from Kent, Ohio. She registered for the Academy of Model Aeronautics Convention held at the Hilton Hotel two weeks ago."

"The hair does not provide absolute identification. But if we can find her workroom where she built the model plane, we can match the pieces of the exploded plane with material in her workshop. In another courtroom situation, a man was convicted of murdering a former girlfriend by sending a bomb through the mail, which exploded upon opening. With reasonable scientific certainty the prosecution was able to show that the particles from the exploded bomb matched materials found in his workshop."

"Look," Jeff said, "I'll check Kent, Ohio, and will be back in touch. I'll also try to get the signed registration form."

There was a dull click at the other end of the line.

Jeff was curious so he went to the Internet and found the Kent, Ohio phone book. He made a list of the various Moores listed as well as the number for Kent State University. There were five Moores, so he went back to his office and called each of the numbers. He was able to call four of the numbers. Jeff then called information at Kent State and got the telephone number of the Psychology Department. There was no Professor Moore on the Psychology faculty.

"So she lied to me," Jeff thought. He decided to try a different tactic altogether. Jeff then called Martinsburg and asked for the names, addresses, and a copy of the tax returns of all taxpayers with the last name of Moore listing themselves as a professor or educator. The computer could do this chore in a short period of time.

As easy as it was to get tax returns, it was surprising that more tax returns were not "leaked to the press." Nixon's tax return was leaked by a dissatisfied IRS employee. Yet, known unlawful disclosures of private citizens' tax returns have been relatively infrequent. The guilty party could go to prison.

The small number of tax disclosures was not due to the lack of opportunity, however. The IRS relies heavily on the integrity of its employees rather than on strict enforcement of security measures. The law requires the IRS and other federal agencies to protect the confidentiality of the taxpayer's data. But Jeff knew that security weaknesses were numerous. Under the computerized data retrieval system, more than 100,000 authorized users had instantaneous access to most taxpayers' records.

The IRS was once powerful and intimidating. David Burnham in *A Law Unto Itself,* describes the IRS as "the single most powerful instrument of social control in the country." A massive computer system makes America's income tax returns available on thousands of terminals scattered throughout the country. IRS employees were able to obtain any tax return for the past five years for any taxpayer in any of the ten regional computer centers.

In recent years, however, the lack of money has restricted spending on tax auditors, criminal investigators, and new technology. Many of the more experienced IRS employees have left or retired in the last five or six years because of onerous paperwork requirements. The IRS estimates that corporate tax cheating with abusive tax shelters cost the government around $123 billion. As many as eight out of ten tax cheaters never pay any taxes, interest, or penalties. Congress has starved the IRS, while giving massive amounts of money to the SEC and the Corporate Fraud Task Force.

Jeff left a note for his secretary to pull any information from the IRS computer files and the Internet about Deidre Moore. It was a long shot. He also asked for any information about any research on subliminal suggestions.

Jeff had made plans to drive out to a Safe House on the outskirts of Baltimore. Several of Nick's informers might provide the reason for his death or the identity of his killer. Jeff could now inquire about an educated, strawberry blonde hit woman.

As he was driving to the Safe House, he remembered his conversation with Henry Silverman. He had forgotten all about Henry after the phone call concerning Deidre Moore. He wondered how valid the information was that Silverman had given him. Silverman had made some serious mistakes, but he was not stupid and didn't forget names or faces. If Richard Onner had been at one of his seminars, Silverman would have remembered. At this point in time, he didn't think Silverman would be doing any more lying. He just wanted to get out of his present situation. Jeff made a mental note to check out Silverman's story at the first opportunity.

For now it was back to the task at hand. He surely hoped that he could get some information at the Safe House. A Safe House is a hideout for defectors, spies, and informers. An individual may need protection or may be in the process of obtaining a new identity. In the sixties this Safe House had been operated by the CIA under the code name, "Operation Midnight Climax." It had been used in mind control experiments. Drug-addicted prostitutes were kept as $100-a-day informers. They slipped LSD and other drugs to unknowing customers while CIA observers recorded what happened.

The Safe House was now used for more legal purposes. Although still operating as a brothel, it was used by various agencies of the government. It came under the Federal Witness Protection Program (FWPP) and was operated by the U.S. Marshal's Service. An individual could be "hidden" at the brothel for a temporary period of time. Or an informer of organized crime might find the Safe House a temporary home before fading away into obscurity or at least trying to disappear permanently.

Neither of his informers could provide Jeff with any leads with respect to Nick's death. Further, no one was aware of a professional hit woman fitting the description Jeff provided.

The trip had been a total waste. The old, two-story home reminded him of the stress seminars he had attended in Chicago as a young agent. The IRS operated the secret school for undercover Special Agents. They tested them with liquor and women to determine if they could resist disclosing their identities. The program had been billed as "stress seminars" for reimbursement purposes.

Buzz—Buzz—Buzz –

Jeff ducked when he heard the sound. It was only a bee. Yet cold sweat rolled down his back. Could he ever get the sound of the destructive airplane out of his mind?

Chapter 15

If taxes are the price we pay for a civilized society, let us be sure they are collected in a civil manner.

                                —Rep. Robin Tallon

"There are similarities between rare coin investing and the over-the-counter stock market. Rare coins on the wholesale market are sold on a bid-and-ask system, similar to the over-the-counter market. Several publications provide a weekly service of providing the bid-and-ask prices of the many coins available to a numismatist. A number of weekly or monthly newspapers, magazines, Internet sites, and newsletters extol the virtues of collecting rare coins." Jack Rosenbaum was giving his standard speech at a Los Angeles coin club.

"A numismatist is a coin or paper money collector. Aside from the many types of coins and dates, a numismatist must worry about a maze of double-die varieties, over-dates, mint errors, three-legged buffaloes, and many other subtle differences. Coin collecting involves an art, which has been practiced for almost two centuries."

"The name Rosenbaum has become synonymous with coin collecting and investing. Rosenbaum, Inc., is the major enterprise in the rare coin business. Rosenbaum is one of a diminishing breed of businesses—the family-owned enterprise."

Of course, Jack Rosenbaum did not include the following facts in his standard speech.

In the mid-'80s Rosenbaum was one of several large companies in the mail-order coin business. At the end of 1990, the rare coin industry went into a severe bear market similar to the 1954–64 coin bull market. Many of the mom-and-pop small retail dealers went out of business. But the coin slump was a blessing in disguise for Rosenbaum, Inc. The youthful president, Jack Rosenbaum, bought out many of these small retail dealers. His father had established the parent coin company many years earlier in Phoenix. After the coin slump Rosenbaum controlled more than 1,500 small retail rare coin outlets.

Slightly portly, Jack Rosenbaum was characteristically dressed in a brown suit. He wore a full black mustache and had neatly parted wavy hair. When not lecturing, however, Jack Rosenbaum ran a tight shop; he told precious little about the business. His taciturnity took second-seat only to his fanatic obsession with profit making. Employees indicated that Jack Rosenbaum was so tightfisted that he rummaged through employees' desks looking for excessive stockpiles of paper clips and pencils.

Rosenbaum, Inc. had two basic operations—mail order and small retail outlets. Many investors were sold coins through his mail-order business located in Phoenix, Arizona. An investor is an individual who purchases a rare coin for the future price increase. He is in the coin market for a profit. An investor generally buys coin rolls or type coins. A type coin is the key coin that is needed in a collection which is composed of one of each coin in a given series.

Rosenbaum, Inc. sold rare coins through the mail like Cal Worthington sells used cars in Los Angeles. At age 89, Cal still owns four dealerships and has sold more than one million cars with his "My Dog Spot" commercials. However, the coins are sold with high markups. Once an investor buys the coin, it's at least five years before the person can sell the coin close to the purchased price. "Buy them cheap, sell them high, and turn that inventory over," was Jack Rosenbaum's philosophy. It worked with heavy advertising.

Rosenbaum, Inc., in essence, was in the business of selling rare coin portfolios. Sales were stimulated by advertising in such media as airline magazines, journals used in the medical profession, and other similar outlets. Thus, its typical customers were those who responded to its sales pitch. These customers had little knowledge of the rare coin market, and the current high price of gold enticed many customers.

Upon a showing of interest by a customer, Rosenbaum mailed the customer an elaborate advertising brochure, which contained a description of the procedures involved in choosing the rare coins. The advertising brochure sent to the customers consistently described the rare coins as an investment. There were comparisons of gains in the stock market with returns from rare coins. Analysis of coin appreciation and similar investment information were provided.

Lifting up a red book, Jack said, "The retail price of coins can be found yearly in the numismatist's bible—the *Red* Book. This book has sold more copies than any other book except the Bible. Weekly or monthly retail price lists can be found in the various numismatic publications such as *Coin World* and *Numismatic News* and on the *Internet*." Jack omitted from his prepared speech that a rare coin buyer cannot sell his coin to a dealer at retail. The only way a buyer can even sell close to retail is through an auction or on the Internet. If sold at an auction, however, the buyer must pay a commission as high as 20%.

Dealers often speak about the possibility of a buyer selling his coins over the Internet. Hundreds of dealers are connected to each other by the Internet in their establishments.

Jack Rosenbaum's voice rose as he said that "the value of a rare coin depends to a certain extent upon the number of coins issued by the government in that particular series. In general, the fewer coins issued of a particular series, the more valuable the coin might be."

"Our huge national debt should cause gold, silver, and rare coins to explode upward." Jack looked around the audience.

The condition of the coin is an important factor in a coin's value. Jack did not mention the problem with grading. The condition of a coin is in the eyes of the beholder. When a dealer sells a coin he will often overgrade the coin to get a higher price for the coin. But when a person tries to sell the same coin to the dealer, the dealer will undergrade the coin. The dealer will try to steal it from him.

Then, of course, there are counterfeit coins. When one coin can sell for more than $400,000, naturally there will be counterfeiters.

There are also "whizzers." A machine is used to brush the coin to simulate mint condition. In other words, an almost uncirculated coin may be whizzed to make it look like an uncirculated coin. An uncirculated coin may sell for as much as 60% more than an almost uncirculated coin.

Some of this uncertainty about coin quality is overcome by buying a plastic encased coin, certified by a grading service, such as Professional Coin Grading Service (PCGS). PCGS has an online price list of 213,982 current coin prices and 13,838,956 historic coin prices based upon the average dealers' asking prices. Their Internet site boasts of 20 million coins graded, commanding a total value of over $20 billion.

Coins may be purchased almost instantaneously over a certified electronic network. These "slab coins," as they are called, are independent third-party certification and encapsulation. They crashed in late 1990 like the first major speculation episode in Holland, called the Tulipomania by economist John Kenneth Galbraith, in the 1630s. At its height, a single tulip bulb traded for the price of two horses and a carriage. But in 2010 and 2011, the bull market was back. However, coins can deteriorate once encapsulated inside a slab, especially copper coins. And the rising gold and silver prices do not raise all boats.

Rosenbaum did not sell these "slab" coins. Rosenbaum, Inc. did not have to resort to counterfeit or whizzed coins. They used a technique called "sliding." The company would purchase a coin in an almost uncirculated condition. Since most of their customers were not coin collectors, many years might go by before the buyer found out that he had been taken. He has bought a "slider," which is worth significantly less than an uncirculated coin. An uncirculated coin is one that has never been placed in circulation. It has luster and has no evidence of wear. A favorite strategy is to place three or four sliders in a roll of coins sold to an investor. The coin roll may be kept many years and exchange hands many times before those "sliders" are found. Many buyers look only at several coins at both ends of the roll before purchasing the roll of coins. Besides, a microscope is needed to accurately ascertain whether a coin is uncirculated.

"Rosenbaum, Inc. has not forgotten about the coin collector. Coin collectors are serviced by our more than 1,500 retail outlets throughout the U.S. They are in small and large cities, from Maine to California, from Michigan to Florida. Rare coins, mint sets, gold coins, silver dollars, coin rolls, commemorative coins, and many other numismatic items are sold from these small shops. Our buyers are school children, businessmen, priests, salesmen, carpenters, or any of the more than 12 million individuals who are devoted to this fine 'cultural hobby.'"

Obviously, Jack did not speak about his inventory problem. Since the inventory turnover was slow, the coins were priced high in the retail outlets. Jack Rosenbaum checked on the small outlets regularly. Either he or two trusted employees visited the shops unannounced, somewhat like the "Undercover Boss" TV series. It was not uncommon for an unkempt Jack Rosenbaum, possibly with a wig or sunglasses, to ring the security bell and then enter a shop to browse around. He would check the security system, cleanliness of the shop, friendliness of the employees, displays of the coin merchandise, and the advertisements in the local papers or telephone book. Obviously their published monthly magazine entitled "The Best Investment: Rare Coins!" had to be prominently displayed. Jack was quite proud of this publication. He personally wrote a "Dear Collector" letter for each issue. Well, he signed the letter; it was written by the editor of the magazine. That's what the editor was paid to do.

As a young man Jack had published. He was, in fact, a lifetime member of the Numismatic Literary Guild. The organization's claim to fame was its yearly award before 1974 of an old 90 pound, gold-painted typewriter to one of its members. Now you get a photograph.

Jack was admitted to the Guild for research he did on the origin of the word "Dixie," the nickname of the South. The Citizens' Bank of Louisiana in New Orleans issued a $10 note printed before the Civil War. These ten-spots with the French word "DIX" (meaning ten) on its reverse became widely circulated in the South. In 1859, a composer by the name of Dan P. Emmett wrote a song which began, "I wish I wuz in de land of the dixes." The song became a hit, and the word dixes became corrupted to "dixie." Thus, a numismatic term gave the South its nickname.

All Rosenbaum shops also had a red, white, and blue sign indicating that an individual should "Buy the Book; Before the Coin." Under another sign were free pamphlets entitled "Ask Us about Coins in IRS-approved IRA Plans." Some retirement programs were now purchasing gold and silver Eagle coins rather than securities.

Often the shop employee did not know that he had been visited. If anything was out of order or something needed attention, he would receive a telephone call the next day, followed by a letter outlining the demerits. Demerits meant a reduction in the shop employer's profit sharing plan at the end of the year. These unannounced visits were effective. They kept the employees constantly on their toes.

Jack continued his lecture. "I am a former-President of the American Numismatic Association. This non-profit organization has the distinction of being one of the few organizations operating under a Federal Charter. The charter was signed by William H. Taft on May 9, 1912. Membership is open to any person 11 years of age or older. The organization provides a numismatic library in its Colorado Springs headquarters, presents awards and prizes, and provides a service of authenticity of numismatic materials submitted by anyone."

"While I was President of ANA, I led a campaign against the Treasury Department and the Bureau of the Mint. I campaigned with the slogan: 'The little man's friend.' My campaign was against the Treasury Department charging so much for the proof and mint sets, which are sold each year.

"A proof set includes one of each type of coin minted during a particular year. The coins are made from carefully selected coin blanks that have been highly polished before being fed into the presses. The coins are hand-fed to a slow-moving press, and each coin is struck twice. The smooth, brilliant, mirror-like reflective surface makes the coin worth much more than even an uncirculated coin.

"A mint set has one coin of each denomination produced by a particular mint in a given year. A mint set has uncirculated coins, but they are not proof-like.

"The Tax Reform Act of 1986 caused an adverse effect upon many tax shelters such as oil and gas, real estate, and movies. These changes encouraged me to diversify. I created a publishing house." Jack did not mention that he owned "The Factory."

Like a pied piper, Jack found a number of followers that evening. "Let the buyer beware" was forgotten by the assembled group. There were no tough or embarrassing questions from the audience. The huge national debt was certainly a prime selling point.

Chapter 16

An income tax form is like a laundry list—either way
you lost your shirt.

—Fred Allen

Richard Onner had one major flaw, which he guarded vigorously. He was tall, slim, and handsome. He did not fit the image of a computer operator. In fact, he was the perfect image of the old-fashioned, straight arrow G-man. He should have been a Special Agent or an FBI agent. He was a good computer operator. But he was a "fanaholic." Since high school, Richard could not sleep unless a fan was running. He needed the constant hum of the fan to drown out any extraneous noise. He told his girlfriends that the fan helped the air conditioner. He said that the circulating air was good for his body and for his sex life. Even when he traveled, Richard carried a small, but noisy fan in his suitcase.

Onner entered the Rosenbaum Coin and Stamp Shop on Saturday morning. The small business was located on Main Street in Martinsburg. There were several teenagers in the shop. Two boys were looking at the inexpensive coins in the two for $1.00 box. A girl wearing braces on her teeth was thumbing through a United States stamp collection.

Onner merely browsed through the shop looking at the various coins in the finger-smudged glass counters. After the buzzer on the door indicated that the last teenager had left. Onner asked, "May I see this 1916 Standing Liberty Quarter?"

"Sure, it's a nice one. It's not often you can find an uncirculated 1916 Quarter," responded the smiling shop manager.

143

Onner knew that the Liberty standing motif had been the victim of censorship. In 1916, the design of the quarter was changed. The new, controversial obverse side of the coin featured Liberty in the form of a goddess who was draped in a sheer gown. The goddess was holding a protective shield in one hand and an olive branch in the other. She was standing at the gate of a parapet. The goddess Liberty, "Heaven Forbid," was shown with her bosom undraped and visible.

This classical pose was short-lived. There was a tremendous public outcry, especially by a number of women's groups. The goddess of Liberty was redesigned midway through 1917. To protect the goddess from onlookers, she wore a heavy vest of armor from 1917 until the coin was discontinued in 1930.

Onner noticed the abbreviation XF and Type 1 written on the coin holder. On the back of the coin holder were the following symbols: ⊔ ⌐ ∟ ⌐ XX. Richard knew the code. The cost of the coin to the dealer was $4,375. The dealer was using a tic-tac-toe-code, derived from the freemasons' cipher created in the 1700s to protect the secrets of this fraternal organization, with one in the top left-hand corner and nine in the bottom right-hand column. An X stood for a zero.

1	4	7
2	5	8
3	6	9

Thus, the symbol ⊔ was four; ⌐ was three; ∟ was seven; ⌐ was 5; and XX was 00.

"I'll take it. I want a written guarantee that the coin is genuine. How much?"

"That'll be $3,950." The shop manager handed Onner a receipt, which contained the following description: 1916 S.L. 25cts, EF, and $3,950. The shop manager also handed Onner the standard guarantee form. He had signed and dated the guarantee and included the description of the coin.

When Onner returned home, he put the coin in a small wall safe behind a false receptacle. Above the wall receptacle was a picture of himself hang gliding. He then picked up the copy of Numismatic News on a coffee table and turned to the appropriate section.

In EF condition the coin was worth about $10,000. Onner smiled, "Not bad for one day's work."

* * *

Jeff had called in sick Friday. He called from Martinsburg. He observed Onner all day Friday. He followed Onner all day Saturday.

It had been necessary for Jeff to call in sick. His group manager had told him to leave the Onner case alone. Another agent was in charge of the investigation. When Jeff asked who, his supervisor said he did not know. Jeff was determined to catch Onner and Nick's murderer. A gut feeling told him that there was some connection between the two.

On Sunday, when he got back to Baltimore, he looked up Rosenbaum in the phone book. Sure enough, there was a Rosenbaum's Rare Coins listed in the yellow pages. There might be a chain of these coin shops.

After lunch on Sunday he went to his office. He spent several hours on the Internet looking through telephone books. He looked in the cities where a major university was located. He looked for the name Deidre Moore. Maybe Deidre was a professor herself. He had no luck.

Jeff looked in the various Who's Who reference books. Nothing!

Shifting his attention to Rosenbaum, Inc., he checked Standard and Poor's Register:

Rosenbaum, Inc.
(Subs Rosenbaum Press)
1010 West Indian School Road
Phoenix, Arizona 85026 602-964-3730

Pres. Jack Rosenbaum
V-P and Secy. Harriet Coupland
V-P and Treas. Harry Fein

*Also Director, Other Directors
Faye Rosenbaum
Jack Rosenbaum, Jr.

Accts. Peat, Anderson & Ernst, LLP.
Sales Range $120 mil. Employees 127
Products: Rare coins, stamps, and books
S.L.C. 3611

He checked the *Directory of Inter-Corporate Ownership.* More than 1,500 small coin and stamp retail outlets were controlled by Rosenbaum, Inc. Strangely, an ammunition plant located in Wickenburg, Arizona, was wholly owned by Rosenbaum, Inc.

Next, Jeff went to the computer console and retrieved the past three corporate income tax returns of Rosenbaum Coin and Stamp Shop in Martinsburg. For the past year the corporation showed a small profit which was offset by net operating loss carryovers, resulting in a refund of $28,600. For the other two years the corporation showed net operating losses of $62,550 and $42,620. "That's fairly large for such a small business," thought Jeff.

Excitedly, he began retrieving each of the tax returns of the other coin outlets on the console. A pattern began to emerge. Most of the outlets showed losses. If they did not show a loss, the profit was minimal.

Also, a number of the shops had been purchased in recent years. Before the coin shops were purchased by Rosenbaum, they normally showed a significant net income. Yet the year after they were purchased, the purchased businesses would show a loss.

After looking at about 200 coin outlets' tax returns, Jeff's eyes felt like they were falling out of their sockets. He took another bite of his Mars bar, and then he retrieved the tax return of the main headquarters in Phoenix. It was a consolidated tax return. The wholesale business showed a tremendous net income. One hundred and twenty million dollars gross profit, with a sixty-two million-dollar net profit. But this net profit was offset on the consolidated tax return by the net operating losses of the various retail outlets. After all adjustments, the wholesale business showed a refund of one hundred and sixty-two thousand dollars.

"Wait a minute," Jeff shouted to himself. He immediately retrieved the tax return of the Martinsburg coin outlet. How can the Martinsburg shop have a net operating loss and receive a tax refund if the wholesale parent company is filing a consolidated tax return? Like a thunderbolt, the answer came to him. He almost shouted, "They can't do both! When a group of affiliated corporations files a consolidated tax return, the parent corporation files the return and receives any refund—not the individual businesses."

Jeff excitedly made some calculations on a piece of paper:

Parent company (.40 x $62M)	$ 24.8M
Subsidiaries (1507 x Average refund of $120,000)	+180.8
	$205.6

"Wow! This company is ripping off more than two hundred million dollars a year from the government!" Jeff whispered to himself. "They're sending in double tax returns. Each outlet sends in a separate return and receives a refund. The parent corporation files a consolidated tax return and receives a refund. The parent corporation files a consolidated tax return and turns its sixty-two million dollars taxable income into a refund of one hundred and sixty-two thousand dollars."

Next Jeff checked to see if the corporations had been audited in the past. None of the retail outlets had been audited in two out of three years. The wholesale business in Phoenix had been audited in two out of the three years. Both years the supervising agent had been Tony Blake.

Why hadn't the retail outlet been audited? Why hadn't the Martinsburg's computer system caught this double counting of losses? It had to be Onner. Somehow he was short-circuiting the internal controls system.

Onner was circumventing the IRS's fail-safe system. Any refund greater than $2 million must be approved by the Joint Committee on Taxation, a Congressional committee. This same committee produced a 1974 study showing that the then President Nixon had underpaid his taxes from 1969 to 1972 by \$476,431. Someone had set up a system whereby the numerous retail outlets received refunds each year of less than \$2 million, but the total refunds for the businesses were a staggering two hundred million dollars.

Each District Office thought that the individual coin shop was being audited with the consolidated parent. Apparently, this agent Tony Blake was either stupid or a crook.

Jeff got up from the computer console and walked around both tense and excited. Jeff wanted to think a minute. He walked over to the window to check his car. There was little traffic tonight.

Jeff looked through the window. He had parked his dirty car on the street under a light. Someone was in the back seat of his car!

Jeff pounded on the window. "Get out of my car!" he screamed. But no one could hear. He was on the fifth floor. He turned and ran to the elevator. Important seconds flew by. It took him about three minutes to get to the front door. He drew his gun as he raced to his car, his adrenaline flowing. Why would a punk break into his car? He had locked it and had left nothing in the car.

No one was there. He looked around. No one. His car doors were still locked. He unlocked the left door and looked into the back seat. Nothing unusual.

Then he saw a small wire leading to the edge of the doorframe. There was something black under the front seat. Jeff remembered the model airplane. He turned and ran with all his might. He dove behind another car.

There was a loud explosion. Pieces from his car were falling around him. His car was on fire. His only car.

Suddenly Jeff knew. A maniac had killed Nick and was now trying to kill him. It had to involve the investigation of Onner. Jeff was shaking when he stood up from his protective spot. He had cheated fate twice. What had caused him to walk to the window at that particular moment? He was still carrying the uneaten portion of the candy bar. He threw it in the street next to a part of his fender.

He had left his cell phone upstairs, so he slowly walked over to an unlit phone booth. The telephone cord had been severed. Typical of Baltimore's telephone system. Jeff cursed. There are few pay phones today.

Twenty minutes later, after calling the police from his office, Jeff gave a description of the drama to the Baltimore police. The fire was still smoldering. A crowd had gathered. The police had theorized that the bomb had been timed to explode about fifteen seconds after the left door was opened.

Jeff asked the policemen to save any remaining pieces of the explosive device. He suggested they call Detective Garrison in Washington, D.C., to coordinate the investigation. He indicated that Nick's death and this bombing were related.

Jeff went home and called Detective Garrison. He related the evening's events, giving the detective the name of the Baltimore policemen who investigated the explosion.

The detective indicated that there was no Deidre Moore living in Kent, Ohio. In fact, no one by the name of Deidre Moore owned an automobile in the United States. He had checked each state looking for an automobile owner by such a name. Jeff told the detective about the possible connection between the bombings and Onner.

Early Monday morning Jeff called Nick's supervisor and asked him who was in charge of the Onner investigation. "I don't know," was the response. "What investigation?"

Jeff explained his suspicions about Onner and Rosenbaum, Inc. "Since this involves a federal employee and my friend Nick was killed, can I help your task force find the guilty parties?"

"Okay," was the simple answer.

Chapter 17

A taxpayer is someone who doesn't have to take a civil service examination to work for the government.

—Anonymous

On his morning flight to Phoenix, Jeff tried to estimate the minimum number of IRS employees who had to be involved in this conspiracy. Jeff knew there were dishonest IRS employees. He himself had padded his expense account. A mail clerk in an IRS center in South Carolina stole 300 IRS refunds in 1987. His intentions were to cash the checks, but he was arrested by police searching for a man who robbed a Pizza Hut.

Robert O. Steven, a Division Director in the IRS, was sentenced to 46 months in prison in 2008 for laundering money for Harriette Walters, a manager in the District of Columbia Office of Tax Revenue. He set up a clothing store, and from 1990 to 2007, Steven and his wife deposited 67 fraudulently obtained District of Columbia government checks or cash amounting to about $9 million that they received as D.C. tax refunds from Walters.

The "Whiskey Ring" prosecutions had revealed corruption in the Bureau of Internal Revenue. An Assistant Treasurer of the United States resigned after revealing that he used inside knowledge of his office to gamble for profit on the gold exchange. A deputy collector in Newark, New Jersey sold taxpayers' addresses for three cents each to a New York business dealing in mailing lists. Even former President Rutherford B. Hayes indicated in his diary that he forgot to file tax returns in 1868 and 1869. But nothing compared to this apparent rip-off.

Jeff decided that Onner was involved, that the auditing revenue
agent, Tony Blake in Phoenix, was involved, and probably the agent's
group supervisor. The group supervisor assigns the taxpayers to
the various agents and double-checks the finished products. "Yes,
a minimum of three employees could pull off such a caper," Jeff
decided. But more people could be involved. IRS employee collu-
sion would negate many of the agency's internal controls. Whom
could he trust in Phoenix?

As the big plane made its approach and descended blindly through
the white clouds, Jeff saw that Phoenix was bordered by mountains
on the north and south and small ranges could be seen in the distance to the west and east. What amazed him was the stark con-
trast of the countryside around Phoenix. Surrounding Phoenix was
lush emerald green landscape from the irrigated farm land. As if
someone had taken a giant knife and cut a circle around Phoenix,
outside this circle began the brown, unimpressive desert from the
sky.

"To your left, folks, you can see the Camelback Mountains, a
famous landmark in Phoenix." Jeff was not impressed by the information furnished by the pilot. To Jeff, the Camelbacks were just
little hills. How could anyone get excited about two little lumps?

Soon after the plane landed on the west runway of the Sky Harbor airport, Jeff went downstairs to retrieve his one suitcase. Pas-
sengers were already pushing and shoving around the silver luggage
carrier. It reminded Jeff of pigs on a farm lined up to get the slop
from the trough. Jeff was tempted to tell one large lady to get out
of his way. But he held his temper.

Next, Jeff rented a compact car and drove north on Freeway 10
and turned left on West Indian School Road. The weather was hot
and dry. Typical desert weather. He noticed the palm trees and the
stately cottonwood trees.

Rosenbaum, Inc., was located in a massive, stark white brick
building. A brightly painted sign indicated that this fortress was
the headquarters of the "Largest Rare Coin Company in the World."
The building had no windows—solid brick. Jeff wondered if a
bazooka could pierce the fortified building.

After leaving his blue car in a nearby parking lot, Jeff walked to the entrance of the building. He noticed a metal grille, which could be slid in front of the door at night. A stately cactus seemed to guard the entrance.

Inside the door Jeff found himself in a small room. A receptionist sat behind a bullet-proof glass wall. There was a television camera focused on Jeff.

"Hello there," came the receptionist's voice over a speaker. "May I help you?"

"Yes, I would like to purchase some rare coins."

"Sir, we do not sell rare coins here. This is our mail order outlet. We do, however, have a retail store at 1711 Main Street. I'm sure that they have whatever you might need."

"Okay, I'll go there."

"That's 1711 Main Street," came the sweet voice over the speaker as Jeff turned and walked to the door.

Jeff checked into a motel and called Rosenbaum, Inc. A voice said, "Hello, Rosenbaum Company."

"I'm Jeff Burke. I have a manuscript dealing with coin collecting. Could I speak to someone in your publishing department?"

"Just a moment."

Country music came over the telephone. Jeff hated to be put on hold. He began to exercise his fingers. First his left hand; then his right hand. He needed to keep his hands in shape for pitching softball. He remembered his injury. He switched to rotating his head, exercising his neck muscles.

The music abruptly stopped. "Hello, I'm Miss Calhoun. So you have a manuscript. What's it about?"

"Silver dollars."

"Mr. Carter is not here today. Could you bring a copy of the manuscript to our office tomorrow at 10:30 a.m.? 1010 West Indian School Road. Ask for Mr. Carter at the door."

"Sure I'll be there."

Jeff then called the IRS office in Phoenix and asked for Tony Blake.

"Hello, this is Tony Blake."

"I'm an accountant for a racketeer in Phoenix involved in vending machines and garbage collection. I'm in trouble and believe I may be eliminated. Could I talk to you about a deal? I could meet you in the lobby of the Ramada Inn on Indian School Road at 9:00 tonight. Will you come?"

"I'm not a Special Agent."

"That's okay. I know you, but you don't know me. Please come alone. I'll talk to a Special Agent at another time. Bring in a milkshake cup from McDonald's in order for me to recognize you. Can you wear a baseball hat?"

"I don't know."

"Please!"

"Okay. I'll be there at 8:30, Is that all right?"

"Yes."

Next Jeff looked for Wickenburg on the map provided by the rental car agency. Route 89 North would take him to the ammunition plant owned by Rosenbaum.

The scenery on the way to Wickenburg was interesting. There were short cacti and tall cacti. He saw a Saguaro. He had read on the plane that a Saguaro cactus takes two hundred years to reach maturity.

This adventure was Jeff's first trip to Arizona. He still remembered the television commercial about giving your sinuses a rest in Arizona. He drove through Surprise, population 58,000. What a strange name for a town.

Near Morristown, the terrain became hilly and the road began to wind. For some distance the road followed the Hassayampa River. He noticed a big bird climbing majestically in the sundrenched air. There was tall galleta grass along the right-hand side of the road.

In semi-desert Wickenburg, population 2,744, Jeff stopped at one of the two service stations and inquired about the location of the ammunition plant.

A darkly tanned attendant wearing cowboy boots was responsive to Jeff's inquiry. "Take Route 60/70 West for about two miles; there's a small road to the left, Vulture Peak Trail. It's between mile markers 19 and 20. When you see a small airport, you've passed the road. Take the country road for about four miles toward Vulture Mine. Cut left on the first side road. Go about five miles. It's near Vulture Peak. Need any gas? Are you going to climb the Peak?"

"No, but I'll fill it up."

Jeff found the small road. Boy, would he hate to get stranded in this place. Vulture Peak did dominate the desert. Jeff had read that the peak was 3,658 feet high. Unconsciously, as he turned on to the road he looked in his rear view mirror to see if anyone was following him. He half expected to see Deidre Moore chasing after him.

Jeff was glad he had his .38 revolver strapped on. Although an agent has the right to carry a weapon while on duty, Jeff hardly ever wore his pistol. But this Deidre Moore affair was making him jumpy.

The strapped weapon near his armpit jogged his memory of the "Cowboy." "Cowboy" had been the nickname of an agent from Texas who had been assigned to the Baltimore office several years ago. He received his nickname from the fact that he always wore his weapon on his side-hip in a holster like a cowboy. One day during the Christmas holidays, Cowboy was shopping with his wife in Baltimore. A young hood tried to rob him with a knife. Cowboy drew his revolver to defend himself. Somehow the robber took the pistol away from Cowboy and shot him with his own gun. Cowboy died.

The Baltimore office would not forget this episode. Some of the agents began to refer to the deceased Cowboy as "quick-draw."

Far ahead on the left side of the road was Vulture Peak—a fairly large mountain for the desert scenery. A huge tumbleweed rolling in front of him brought his attention back to the rough road. Shortly before Jeff reached Vulture Peak, he turned left onto a gravel road. His compact car began to strain as the elevation increased. The landscape was covered with small bushes, with gullies here and there.

Ahead was a small sign: "Rosenbaum Ammunition. No Admittance." The plant was surrounded by a tall metal fence. About every fifty feet on the fence was a sign that said "Danger: No Admittance."

Jeff drove to the guard house. "Hi, I'm a reporter from the *Phoenix News*. We are doing a story on the ammunition plant and its impact on Arizona's economy. Could I take a tour of the plant?"

"Sorry, no one's admitted. We don't give tours," was the rough reply from the heavy-set guard.

"What's your name? Do you realize I can write either a favorable or an unfavorable article about your employer?"

"Look, mister, do you see that sign? It means no admittance. Turn your car around and don't come back here unless you have a signed letter from the plant supervisor."

"Who is he?"

"Call and find out," was the curt response.

Jeff turned the car around and left. He did not want to argue with a moron guard holding a weapon.

Once back in Wickenburg, Jeff stopped at Harvey's Diner. Jeff sat down at the counter and ordered some chili. It was a spiced stew of ground beef and minced chilies—diarrhea food, for sure.

After some casual conversation with Harvey, the owner, Jeff asked, "What do they do at the plant near Vulture Peak?"

"You're new here, huh? Are you a Yankee?"

"Yes, just driving through."

"They make ammunition."

"Why is it just stuck out there in the desert?"

Harvey looked at Jeff as if he were dumb. "Do you realize what would happen if the place were to catch on fire? They also make some bombs. They made a lot of bombs during the Vietnam war. Rumor was that they were going to make the neutron bomb here, but Peanut Carter killed that. I have some land near Vulture Peak. I would be rich now if they had been able to make the neutron bomb here. Do you want to look for some gold? For twenty dollars, I'll let you look for gold on my land."

Harvey reached behind the counter and showed Jeff a rock. "See that? That's a gold nugget from my land. I'll rent you a gold detector. It will detect a single speck of gold no larger than a pinhead.

"I also have a dowsing detector. It's a directional locator. The early Spanish settlers used dowsing instruments to locate gold and silver deposits in Mexico. Our boys used this triangulation method to find V.C. land mines in Vietnam.

"Henry Wickenburg discovered gold at Vulture Mine in 1863. This town grew as a gold mining camp. The mine produced millions of dollars of gold. But Henry Wickenburg died a pauper; he killed himself.

"How about it? Do you want to look for some gold?"

"No, I don't have time. Where's your bathroom?" Jeff asked.

* * *

Jeff was more interested in silver—silver dollars, that is. Jeff had watched Tony Blake arrive at the Ramada Inn wearing a baseball hat the night before with a milkshake cup. Jeff had not approached him, but he had observed him at a distance. After about forty-five minutes Tony Blake had left, a little angry. This whole charade was to determine what Tony looked like.

At 10:30 a.m. Jeff arrived at the entrance of Rosenbaum, Inc. He entered the small room separated by a glass wall from the receptionist.

"Hello, I'm here to see Mr. Carter about writing a book. I'm Jeff Burke."

"Just a moment."

The receptionist called someone on her phone. After a few brief remarks which Jeff could not hear, she looked up and pressed a button which caused a buzzing sound in the glass wall.

"You may come in, Mr. Burke. Go through the door and turn left. Follow the wall to the door on the left labeled Publications. Mr. Carter is in a conference now, but he should be out in a moment."

Inside was a large room with many employees. Around the outside of the room were a number of small offices. The front of each office was enclosed by glass except for a wooden door leading into each office.

Jeff immediately noticed that many of the employees had weapons on their desks. Not your ordinary paperweight! A pistol here, a rifle there, next was a pump shotgun. There were several gun racks on the walls with weapons. "Good grief," Jeff thought, "this place must be Fort Knox."

Jeff followed the wall for a while, but turned right before reaching the door marked Publications. He walked past about thirty people in what looked like enlarged telephone booths. Each person seemed to be talking about a gold coin, another about a "key" coin. A young woman was talking about the explosive investment potential of rare coins.

Ahead was an office not enclosed by a glass front. On the door in large letters was

Jack Rosenbaum
President

A secretary sat near the entrance of the door. Jeff approached the busy lady and said, "I would like to speak to Mr. Rosenbaum." Jeff had not planned to act as an agent here. He merely wanted to look around. But at this moment Jeff decided that he wanted to try to get inside the ammunition factory.

She looked up, surprised, and asked, "Do you have an appointment?"

"No, but I believe Mr. Rosenbaum will speak to me." Jeff showed her his "Special Agent, Treasury Department" card.

Without hesitation the secretary dialed two numbers and said, "Mr. Rosenbaum, there is an IRS agent out here who wishes to speak to you."

In several seconds a tall, portly man with a precisely trimmed black mustache bounced out of the door smiling. But as soon as he saw Jeff his smile disappeared.

"Uh, hello. What can I do for you?"

Jeff decided that Jack Rosenbaum had expected to see Tony Blake. "Oh, nothing important. Tony Blake just asked me to drop by and say hello. He wants me to go over your tax records of the ammunition plant."

"Won't you come in," Jack said as he pointed toward his door. "Could I see your identification? You know we can't be too careful with as many robberies as there are in Phoenix."

Jeff handed Jack his credentials. Jack studied them for a few moments and gave them back to Jeff.

Before Jeff went into the office, another gentleman exited and walked toward the front entrance.

Jeff entered the spacious office, and Rosenbaum motioned for Jeff to sit down at a small table on the front side of Jack Rosenbaum's mammoth oak desk. Jeff noticed that a Remington shotgun and a bolt-action Remington rifle with a leather sling rested within easy reach of Jack's chair behind his desk.

On Jack's desk was a picture of an attractive lady and two boys. On one wall was a framed dollar bill with the caption, "My first dollar," followed by the signature, Jack Rosenbaum. Also on the wall was a sign:

"Impossible is a word to be found only in the dictionary of fools."

—Napoleon

Jack was the first to break the uncomfortable silence. "Of course, we do not keep any records concerning our ammunition factory here. They are kept at the plant in Wickenburg."

"Yes, I drove out there, and they would not let me enter. Could I get a written statement from you allowing me to look at those records?"

Jack pressed an intercom button and said, "Molly, would you type a statement to the effect of allowing Mr. Burke, is it Jeff?" nodding to Jeff.

"Yes."

"It's Mr. Jeff Burke—giving him permission to look at our records at the Wickenburg plant. I'll sign it. Address it to Barry Schapiro."

"Are there any problems?" Jack eyed Jeff for an answer. "No, not really. I'm going to start helping Tony Blake do some auditing of your tax return. I want to start with the ammunition plant in order to get a *larger* refund." Jeff was trying to get some incriminating evidence from Jack Rosenbaum.

"I don't understand. I thought IRS agents always tried to get more money from us. Is this a new policy?"

"Mr. Rosenbaum, I have talked to Tony. I understand the arrangement. You have nothing to fear from me."

"Seriously, Mr. Burke, I do not understand what you are talking about. What 'arrangement' are you referring to?" Rosenbaum's right hand smoothed his black mustache.

At that moment the secretary walked in carrying a letter which she handed to Jack.

"Thank you, Molly. Was Tony Blake the young IRS agent that audited our tax return last year?"

"Yes, I believe he was. Do you want me to check the files?"

"No, that won't be necessary." Jack read the short letter and then said, "The letter is fine, Molly."

Molly turned and left the room.

"Mr. Burke, there must be some mistake. You must have our firm mistaken with another company. Mr. Blake did audit our return last year, but found only some minor changes. I believe we had what is called a 'clean return.' I will be glad to call our counsel in here and let you discuss this matter with him." Jack rose to indicate that the interview was finished.

"No, that will not be necessary. I'll talk to Tony." Jeff rose and shook Jack's strong hand. "Could I have the permission letter?"

Jack gave Jeff the letter, and Jeff made a graceful exit.

Jeff drove away for a short distance, but returned to a parking lot across the street from the coin company. He entered a bookstore directly across the street and began to watch the parking lot and the coin company entrance.

Jeff's instincts had been correct. Within an hour, Tony Blake arrived and entered the coin company. He stayed for about twenty minutes and left.

Jeff followed him in his rental car. The revenue agent took Route 89 North to Wickenburg. Jeff followed at a safe distance until they passed through Wickenburg and the agent turned onto the small road which led to Vulture Peak and the ammunition plant. Jeff waited about five minutes until Tony was out of sight, and then he drove toward the ammunition plant. A jack rabbit dashed across the road and the dust and heat was irritating to Jeff's eyes.

When Jeff spotted the ammunition plant, he parked in a side parking lot and waited. After an hour's wait Jeff saw Tony leave the plant, get in his white car, and drive toward Wickenburg.

Jeff locked his car and walked to the entrance of the plant. He gave Rosenbaum's letter to a broad-shouldered guard and asked for instructions on how to locate the main office.

The guard read the letter, turned and went to the small guard-house and made a phone call.

The guard came back and said, "I'm sorry, but we had a personal phone call from Mr. Jack Rosenbaum, and he indicated that you are not allowed to enter. Do you have a summons or search warrant?"

Jeff shook his head and almost shouted, "What is wrong with this company? I have a letter from your president, and you still will not allow me to enter. You people will pay through the nose."

"Sorry," was the response. "We are not sure you are a Revenue Agent. I have called the Wickenburg police so please stay until they arrive. Maybe then we can clear up this matter."

Jeff turned to walk away. Jeff heard the guard draw his gun from his holster.

"Please halt or I'll shoot."

Jeff continued to walk. It was a gamble.

"Halt! If you do not stop, I'll shoot," the guard shouted.

The guard did not shoot. Jeff was perspiring when he reached his hot car.

Jeff was able to catch up with Tony, and he followed the agent for the rest of the day. He followed him home and watched his house until 10:30 that evening.

Chapter 18

There will come a time when the poor man will not be able to wash his shirt without paying a tax.
　　　　　　　　　　　　　　　—A congressman in 1790

The next morning Jeff was watching as Tony left his home and drove to the Federal Building on North First Avenue. Jeff followed him to his IRS office.

Around noon Tony left his office and drove to the Pepper Tree. Once inside Jeff saw that it was a very large building with a variety of restaurants. There were Mexican, Italian, Chinese, German, a deli, and many other small diners and restaurants. Tony ordered a roast beef sandwich at the deli and sat down.

Jeff purchased a small sausage pizza and a glass of light beer. He sat down about two tables away from the agent. Shortly Jeff put his hand to his head to shield his face. He saw Jack Rosenbaum come over and place his tray of Chinese food on Tony's table. They began to talk softly. Jeff could not understand what they were saying, but the expressions on their faces indicated they were angry.

They began to glance and talk to a gentleman wearing dark sunglasses and a straw hat sitting alone at a table next to them. It was not a casual conversation. The man talking to them was vaguely familiar to Jeff, but he could not place the face.

Jeff wished he had an electronic device to overhear the conversation. Of course, Jeff knew the use of a mechanical, electronic, or other device to overhear or record a non-telephonic conversation had to be with the consent of at least one party to the conversation. Further, such activity must be approved in advance by the

Attorney General. A court order or search warrant is not needed for
the transmission or recording of a conversation when done with
the consent of one of the parties. But different states have different laws.

Jeff casually walked over and purchased another light beer. From
the small restaurant, he had a good view of the third man. Jeff took
a small surveillance camera and snapped several shots of the third
person.

Abruptly, the third man rose and walked toward the exit carrying a briefcase. Jeff followed him on a hunch. Outside, the man
hailed a taxi. Jeff noted the number on the taxi and raced to his car.

Jeff was able to catch up with the cab and follow it to the airport. The taxi stopped in front of the Delta Airlines terminal, and
the man wearing the sunglasses and hat went into the terminal.

After he parked his car, Jeff rushed into the same terminal. But
he could not find the unknown man with the briefcase. He had
disappeared. Jeff walked around the Sky Harbor airport for more
than an hour.

But no luck. The only faint ray of hope was the film in his camera. Now he had two mysteries. He was looking for a hit woman with
the name of Deidre Moore. He also wanted to know the name of
the man who disappeared into the airport.

Jeff was at his wit's end. He did not know what to do. He returned his rental car and bought a ticket to Lexington, Kentucky.
One of the newspaper clippings found by his secretary indicated
that a Professor Paul Gregory in the Psychology Department at the
University of Kentucky had conducted some subliminal research
in the early '80s. His secretary had not found any clippings or material concerning Deidre Moore.

The quiet, soft-spoken Dr. Paul M. Gregory indicated that he
had conducted a number of classroom experiments in 1985 and
1986 on subliminal suggestions.

The elderly, thin professor sat behind his desk in his modest
book-cluttered office, and he described his experiments and results
to Jeff. Jeff listened politely, noticing the numerous accomplish-

ments, certificates, and educational degrees that were framed and hung on the white walls.

"I published the results of my experiments in several journals so almost anyone could have read about them," continued the professor.

"That's interesting," replied Jeff as he rubbed the tip of his nose. "Do you have a list of the students who participated in your experiment?"

"That's some time ago," shrugged the professor. "We only have to keep exams for two years."

Professor Gregory slid his chair back, put on his glasses, and walked over to one of the bookcases that was crammed with books.

"But you are lucky. I have a record of every grade I have given. That would be around 1985," the professor mumbled to himself. He searched through a number of grade books. "Ah, here it is," he said as he turned around smiling. "Six classes participated in that particular experiment—about 360 students. I've thrown away their questionnaires, but I do have the names of the participating students. I could photocopy the names of these students. Of course, I can't give you their grades. That would be against the law."

"The names are fine," replied a delighted Jeff. "Do you have the student yearbooks for 1985 and 1986?"

"No, but you might find them in the campus library archives."

Jeff took a copy of the list of students and almost ran to the library. He found the 1985 and 1986 student yearbooks in the library. He began looking at the photographs of each of the students in Professor Gregory's roll book.

After about two hundred and seventy photographs, Jeff saw her— Debra Sweeney. She was a woman in her early twenties, Jeff guessed. She was the Deidre Moore for whom he was searching. Jeff's hands began to shake slightly and his palms became sweaty. She was an ordinary, attractive woman. He remembered that night well.

Jeff pulled out the map to the University of Kentucky's campus, found the location of the Alumni Office, and ran part of the way to the office. He hardly noticed the students going to and from classes.

"Hi, I'm Jeff Burke, a former student. I'm looking for the current address of one of my classmates, Debra Sweeney. Can you help me?"

The lady rewarded Jeff with a smile. "Oh, we probably can bend the rules for a nice young man like you. Let me look in our files."

After several minutes she returned with her perpetual smile. "She now lives in Pikeville, Kentucky. I've written her address and telephone number down." She handed an envelope to Jeff. "Would you take this envelope and consider making a donation to the University? It takes a lot of money to send a student to college now."

Jeff took the envelope and said, "I'll check with my wife. She controls the budget."

When Jeff arrived on his flight to Lexington, Kentucky, he rented another compact car and drove to Pikeville, Kentucky, a three-time All-Kentucky city. The eastern Kentucky coal town has a population of about six thousand, five hundred year round. Each year around 100,000 self-proclaimed hillbillies came to town to celebrate Hillbilly Days. This Model City is laid out like a winding snake along the Chesapeake and Ohio Railroad. Although it was late in the evening, Jeff located Debra Sweeney's two-story house. On the mailbox with black letters was "John Sweeney."

Later in the evening Jeff called one of the guys on his softball team and asked him to check the Internet. "I'll call you around 9:45. Let me know any information about John and Debra Sweeney, 1121 Shady Lane, Pikeville, Kentucky."

Next, Jeff called Rick Garrison, the Washington detective. Jeff said that he needed help in following the suspect since she could recognize him. The detective indicated that he would be in Pikeville sometime tomorrow.

The telephone conversation the next morning with his third baseman provided Jeff with the information that 1) John Sweeney was a Baptist minister, 2) Debra Sweeney was a housewife, 3) they reported a moderate amount of taxable income, 4) their two children were away at college, and 5) Debra reported a modest amount of royalty income from children's books.

As he waited in his car near her house surrounded by beautiful mountains, Jeff wondered if he had been mistaken about the photograph in the yearbook. Maybe she had a twin sister. At 11:45 a.m. Debra Sweeney emerged from her home. Watching with small binoculars, Jeff saw Debra Sweeney wearing striped slacks, a blue blouse, a navy jacket and leather boots come out of her home. She drove towards Pikeville. The woman looked just like the lady he had stayed with at the Hilton convention.

Debra stopped at a phone booth on the way to town and made a short telephone call. Not many phone booths left. Jeff wondered why she did not use a disposable phone. Old school maybe. Jeff noted the time and the location of the phone booth. She then drove to the Baptist Church and went to lunch with her husband, apparently. She certainly did not fit the profile of a professional killer.

The First Bank and Trust was the only bank in Pikeville. The manager was quite surprised when Jeff indicated that he wanted to see the bank records of John and Debra Sweeney.

"Do you mean Reverend John Sweeney?" was the puzzled response.

"Yes," was Jeff's simple answer.

Jeff spent several hours checking signature cards, deposit slips, ledger sheets, teller's proof sheets, safe deposit records and other records. He found nothing out of the ordinary. Rev. and Mrs. Sweeney seemed to be a typical American family living in a small town. In three years, he found only two overdrawn checks—certainly no Bert Lance.

Debra Sweeney had deposited some rather large checks, normally at the end of March and September of each year. Jeff reasoned that these amounts were royalties from her children's books. He noted, also, the rather large checks written to support the two children in college. The son was at Princeton, and the daughter was enrolled in Yale.

Rather disappointed, Jeff left the bank and intended to go back to the motel. Instead he stopped off at the county public library on College Street. He noticed the "Please Be Quiet" sign as he entered the old library. The sign was not heeded. The library was located in the YMCA, and kids were running around shouting and arguing.

A rather elderly lady was behind the counter. She looked up from her book when Jeff said, "May I see several books written by Debra Sweeney?"

"Oh, our only author in Pikeville. Sure, we have them over there on display." The stoop-shoulder lady pointed to four books that were prominently on display. She immediately began reading her romance novel again.

Jeff walked over to the four books on display. He was not impressed. They were short. But aren't all children's books short? "She makes money off of these easy books. Maybe I should start writing children's books," Jeff thought.

He jotted down the publishers of the books. Three of the books were published by Kids Publishing Co. (New York) and the other book was published by Banage Publishing Co. (New York). Jeff went back to his plain motel room at Days Inn and waited. At 4:30, Detective Rick Garrison arrived. Garrison was a tall man in his mid-thirties. As he removed his rumpled overcoat, dandruff fell from his untidy blond hair. A restless, gregarious detective, he grinned as he shook Jeff's hand in a firm grip. His hand was callused and hard like a laborer's.

"How are you, Mr. Burke? Have you found your killer?"

"I believe so. The real name of the woman who picked me up in Washington is Debra Sweeney. She's the wife of a Baptist minister. She doesn't look like a professional killer. Maybe her hair just happened to be on the model plane which hit Nick," shrugged Jeff. "I just don't know. She writes books for children."

"Where does she live?"

"1121 Shady Lane. We'll go out there now. You follow me. I'm going to try to get a flight back to Baltimore tonight. There's not much I can do here. If she sees me with you, that will blow your cover. What do you suggest we do?"

"Well, I suppose follow her for several days. If she did it, someone is paying her. We need to find out who hired her. I'll put a tap on her phone. I will want to get into her home and get some materials from her workroom."

"By the way, on the way into town today to meet her husband, she stopped at a pay telephone and made a call. Did you get a copy of her handwriting at the Hilton?"

"Yes," replied Rick.

"Good," replied Jeff. "We can force her to produce handwriting exemplars to prove she was in Washington. The Fifth Amendment will not shield her from the compelled production of handwriting or voice exemplars."

After showing Rick the Sweeneys' house and the telephone booth, he ate baby back ribs at the Days Inn. Jeff hit patches of ice and snow on his drive back to Lexington, Kentucky. The snowcapped peaks of the mountains did not look inviting. He was able to get a flight into Dulles.

After waking from a short nap, Jeff felt better. Sleep had removed some of the fatigue from his face. He had arrived at the Dulles airport very early in the morning. But by the time he hit his bed, he was asleep.

At 10:00 the next morning when he got back to his office, several of his agent friends were grinning. He should have guessed. Above his desk next to his framed motto by Thomas Edison: "Genius is 99% perspiration and 1% inspiration," was a new addition. During his absence he had been awarded the infamous Special Agent's oath. The oath read as follows:

> I am proud to be a Special Agent. I will be true to the trust and will fulfill the responsibilities placed in me by the Service and my Country. I will dedicate myself to the policies of the Service and in all my activities will uphold the provisions of the Constitution of the U.S.

The Oath had a rough history. Initially, each Special Agent had been given a framed copy of the oath to improve the morale of the Special Agents. But the oath became a laughing joke among the agents. Eventually the group supervisors took back the oath from each agent. Instead, each office got one copy to be given each week to the best agent for the past week.

Even the weekly award did not work. The agents did not want to receive the award. So if an agent was out of the office for several days, he would come back and find the oath over his desk. Jeff would have to find out which of the agents was out of the office today and hang the oath above the missing agent's desk.

His desk had a pile of mail. Included in the stack of correspondence was a fingerprint report on the practice run of the gambling numbers which he had found in the garbage dumpster. He forwarded the report to Hank Brown. Jeff wondered if Hank had found any incriminating evidence on Flesher's porno bookstore and aircraft business.

Jeff had just glanced through a second *Tax Notes* when the phone rang. "Hello," answered Jeff. He suppressed a yawn.

"Hi, Jeff, would you come into my office?" It was Jeff's supervisor, Sam Westley.

"Sure," was Jeff's response.

Sam was Jeff's boss. He was a typical product of the Civil Service System. Sam had not been an outstanding agent. He merely had seniority. He was promoted because the time-in-grade indicated that it was time for him to be promoted. Since Sam was only an average agent, he had stayed out of trouble. He never found any fraud cases which always slowed the productivity of an agent. Thus, when Sam's supervisor had retired, Sam was a non-controversial replacement.

Sam was the epitome of the "Peter Principle." In any organization, an individual is promoted until he reaches his level of incompetence.

On the way to Sam's office, Jeff dropped off the film that he had taken in Phoenix to be developed. He knocked on Sam's office door and then entered.

Even before he sat down, Sam looked up and asked, "Where have you been?"

"Well, I flew to Phoenix to check on the Rosenbaum Coin Company and on the way back I stopped off in Kentucky. I may have found Nick's killer."

"Did it have to do with the Onner affair?"

"Yes, I believe all of these people are involved in a conspiracy to...."

"I thought I told you to drop the Onner affair," Sam barked back. Sam was clearly angry and upset.

Jeff shot back, "Look, Nick was my friend. You would not even tell me who was placed in charge of Nick's investigation." Jeff's scowl indicated that he was as angry as Sam.

Jeff's aggressive outburst apparently decreased Sam's hostility. Calmly, Sam replied, "Look, Rosenbaum made some significant political contributions during the last campaign. Some powerful individuals owe him favors."

"I hate to do this, but I'm suspending you for at least two weeks. I have to do this." In a softer voice he said, "If you leave this affair alone, I believe I can get you reinstated in two weeks. You have a good record. Don't blow it. Let the cops find Nick's murderer. Leave the Rosenbaum and Onner affair alone."

Jeff turned and walked out. He was stunned. Someone extremely important in the IRS was involved. Why else would so much pressure be placed on Sam? Jeff did have a good record and normally had a good relationship with Sam.

Back at his desk, Jeff called Nick's supervisor. "Hello, this is Jeff Burke, Nick's friend. I called you last week indicating my suspicions that Richard Onner, an IRS employee, and the Rosenbaum Coin Company were somehow connected with Nick's death. I now have found enough fraud to close down the Rosenbaum operations. I have a photo of an IRS agent meeting with Jack Rosenbaum and an unknown person in Phoenix."

"I would like to inventory Onner's safe deposit box and audit the Rosenbaum coin shop in Martinsburg. I believe Onner buys rare coins from the company each week. But I've been suspended for at least two weeks. Someone high up in the IRS is trying to shut me up. By the way, I left Washington Detective Garrison in Pikeville. He is shadowing a woman we believe is Nick's killer. Could you meet me at 2:00 at the Martinsburg Bank and Trust, 1210 Main Street?"

"Yes, I'll be there."

Next, Jeff called Kids Publishing Company in New York. After going through the switchboard, he was finally connected to an employee in the accounting department. He found out that Debra Sweeney earned little royalties from the children's books. She earned less than three hundred dollars per year.

His conversation with Banage Publishing Company was even more informative. This company was a vanity publisher. True, the company published her other children's book, but she paid them to publish them.

Jeff reasoned that Debra Sweeney was using the children's books as a money laundering scheme to hide her outside, illegal payments. Maybe she was a professional killer after all.

Chapter 19

The tax code is the single greatest source of lobbying activity in Washington.

— Richard K. Armey

At 2:30, Jeff met Nick's supervisor, Jason Pabst, inside the front door of the Martinsburg Bank and Trust. He had waited for the strike force supervisor for thirty minutes. IRS strike forces are directed toward the identification and investigation of taxpayers who derive substantial income from organized criminal investigation.

Outside the bank the temperature was 31 degrees and falling in a cold wind. Jeff recalled reading that some people are habitually late because they are expressing an unconscious hostility. The individual shows how unconsciously angry he is by forcing the other person to wait. Since Jeff really didn't know the supervisor, Jeff assumed that he was not angry with him.

"Hello, Jeff."

"Hi."

"Sorry I'm late. I ran into some heavy traffic on the way here. Have you talked to anyone?"

"No, as a suspended IRS agent I need your authority," answered Jeff. "I did make an appointment with the manager, Mr. Michaelson, for 2:00."

Jason did not look like an IRS agent. He was short, plump, and slightly balding. He looked like an ordinary accountant rather than a strike force agent charged with the responsibility of finding corruption within the federal government.

"Okay, let's go to work." Jason turned, walked over, and spoke to a woman behind the nearest desk. "Where is Mr. Michaelson?"

"He's in the second office right over there," pointing to the right side of the bank lobby. "You'll have to ask his secretary."

"Hello," Jason said to the attractive, brunette secretary.

"Could we please speak to Mr. Michaelson?"

"Do you have an appointment?"

"Yes. Mr. Burke made an appointment for two o'clock. Obviously, we are late, but I ran into some difficult traffic. I'm Mr. Pabst. This is Mr. Burke," said Jason turning toward Jeff.

The brunette looked at the telephone lights. "Mr. Michaelson is on the phone. Would you wait in those seats? He'll be with you in a moment."

By the time Jason and Jeff had sat down, the secretary picked up the phone and buzzed the manager. "Mr. Burke and Mr. Pabst are here to see you."

Even before the secretary had hung up the phone, the manager came striding out of his office.

"Hi there, I'm Brett Michaelson. Won't you come in." He led Jason and Jeff into his office.

"Mr. Michaelson, I'm Jason Pabst and this is Jeff Burke. I'm an IRS agent with the Treasury Department. We suspect one of your customers, Richard Onner. We'd like to inventory his safe deposit box."

"You or your employees are not to inform Mr. Onner of this inventory. We will need one of your employees to stay with us to ascertain that we do not take anything from his box. Are there any questions?"

"Is this legal? Do you have a written request?"

"Yes, it is legal. Here is a written request." Jason handed the manager a written letter. He read it rapidly and turned and put it on his desk. "I will observe you myself."

When the big box was opened, Jeff whistled softly when he saw so many rare coins. At the top of the box was a list of rare coins with the dates of purchase. There was a sale column. Entries had been made in this column for some of the coins. Most of the coins had been purchased from Rosenbaum Coin and Stamp Shop on Main Street.

They immediately began a written inventory showing the date of entry, box number, name of bank, and owner. In the presence of the manager they made a list of all the rare coins. There were several rare stamps in the box. Once the inventory was taken, Jeff took several photographs of the entire contents. The manager was requested to initial all pages of the inventory and to sign the last page as acknowledgment that the contents were returned to the rental box. They made a copy of the list of coins that had apparently been prepared by Onner.

After thanking the manager for his cooperation and encouraging his silence, Jason and Jeff left. Outside the bank Jason said, "I think we should hit the Rosenbaum Coin Shop now."

"I agree," smiled Jeff. They went directly to the Rosenbaum Coin and Stamp Shop on Main Street.

As they entered the coin shop, Jeff noticed a new sign: "If you don't know your coins, know your dealer! Rosenbaum cares!"

The smiling shop manager greeted them warmly. "May I help you?"

Jason returned the smile and said, "I'm an IRS agent for the Treasury Department. We would like to see your invoices involving any rare coins or stamp sales to Mr. Richard Onner. We are here at closing time so that we will not disrupt your business. However, we would like for you to get these invoices this evening." Jason flashed his Treasury Commission.

The smile disappeared from the shop manager's face. "But I'm going to a play tonight!"

"If you hurry and get those invoices, you'll be able to see it."

"How do I know you are really Treasury Agents? You may be crooks."

Jason took out his card again and handed it to the manager. "Jeff, let him see your badge." Jeff handed the manager his badge.

"I believe I should call my lawyer," the manager replied in a broken voice as he read the cards.

"Look, we just want to see a few invoices. If you give us any trouble, we'll get a court order and audit your whole blasted store. What's it going to be—a little trouble or some *real* trouble?"

Reluctantly the manager turned and went into a back room. Jason and Jeff followed him. He pulled several boxes down from a shelf.

"You're lucky. I give all of my customers a written guarantee, and I file them in alphabetical order." He gave Jason a stack of papers.

"Great, do you have a copy machine? We'll pay you for the copies."

"Yes."

"Also, could you give us the invoices for a customer whose name begins with an S or a T?" They wished to determine the normal mark-up on the coin sales.

Although the shop manager looked puzzled, he gave Jason a small stack of invoices for a customer with the last name of Stern.

Once copies were made of the invoices, Jeff purchased a copy of *Numismatic News.* They left the coin shop and found a motel. That evening, Jason and Jeff prepared a schedule showing the list price, the value of the rare coins on the sale date, and the difference. In each case, they noticed that Onner had been able to obtain a nice paper profit on each purchase. On only those items which they looked up in the *Numismatic News* newspaper, Onner had made a paper profit of about $47,715. The profit would probably eventually be tax-free.

The profit was not really paper profit. Of the rare coins which Onner had purchased from Rosenbaum, he had sold about one third of them. He had made a nice profit on each of these sales.

Jason and Jeff noticed that the coin shop would often list the coin sold to Onner as an almost uncirculated coin (AU-50 or EF-40), whereas the rare coin was listed as uncirculated (UNC or MS-63) on the coin holder.

Jason collected coins. He told Jeff that an uncirculated coin is a newly minted coin which shows no evidence of circulation, but is not necessarily brilliant. A coin can have some nicks and scratches and still be uncirculated. Abrasions may occur when the struck coin falls into the hopper or when the coins are bagged for shipment. More abrasions may occur outside the mint from roll-wrapping techniques and coin-counting machines used by banks. As a general rule, the heavier the coin, the more scratches and nicks it may have.

Jason explained to Jeff that the grade of a coin has a significant effect on its price. For example, an uncirculated MS-63 1846 Lib-

Coin With Grade	*Invoice*	*Price*	*Profit*
1793 Wreath Cent (XF-40)	$3,050	$12,500	$9,450
1795 Flowing Hair Half dime (AU-50)	1,600	9,450	7,850
1806 Draped bust Half dollar (AU-50)	1,800	5,300	3,500
1814 Caped bust, small date Dime (AU-50)	120	1,250	1,130
1802/1 $2 gold piece (AU-50)	3,990	9,000	5,010
1873 Three dollar gold (XF-40) (Closed date)	4,760	6,000	1,240
1894-O $5 gold piece (AU-50)	425	625	200
1875-CC $20 gold piece (MS-60)	640	4,750	4,110
1875-CC $20 gold piece (XF-50)	570	2,650	2,080
1815 Capped bust quarter (AU-50)	1,005	1,750	745
1942/1 Overdate Mercury dime (AU-55)	275	2,250	1,975
1937-D 3-legged Buffalo nickel (AU-55)	230	1,950	1,720
1919 Walking Liberty half dollar (AU-55)	75	1,100	1,025
1892-S Barber half dollar (AU-50)	75	710	635
1920-S Walking Liberty half dollar (AU-55)	35	750	715
1794 Flowing hair half dime (XF-40)	995	7,325	6,330
	$19,645	$67,360	$47,715

erty Seated dollar (tall date) may sell for $2,100 whereas the same coin in almost uncirculated (AU-50) condition may sell for only $250. "Obviously Onner is being paid by the Rosenbaum company through purchases of rare coins at a steep discount. Or Onner is paying the price of an almost uncirculated coin, but is receiving a more valuable uncirculated coin. When Onner needs money, he merely sells the rare coins to other dealers at much higher prices."

Jeff then explained to Jason how all of the 1,500 coin shops were obtaining illegal refunds. How no one was auditing the small coin shops.

Jason was silent for a moment. Jeff noticed that Jason seemed to look to the right when thinking. Jeff knew that this trait indicated that the left hemisphere of Jason's brain was dominant. A left-hemisphere dominance indicated that Jason had a pleasant and optimistic view of life. A person with a right-hemisphere dominance was more prone to depression.

After Jeff explained again to Jason how the many coin shops were obtaining illegal refunds, Jason agreed with Jeff that they had enough evidence to close the whole organization down. "We certainly have enough evidence to get Onner," Jason indicated. "But there are people much higher up in the IRS organization involved if they can force your supervisor to suspend you. Suppose we sit tight, do nothing until we hear from the Washington detective. Maybe your hit woman will lead us to the guilty parties."

Chapter 20

The first great commandment is, don't let them [IRS agents] scare you.

—Elmer Davis

His drive back to Baltimore was uneventful. There was a chill in the wind. He only occasionally glanced at the bare branched trees whipping by his car.

Jeff was up early the next morning. He didn't know why. He had read that short sleepers were energetic, ambitious people who worked hard and kept busy. They did not worry. Jeff was worried. He wondered if he would get his job back.

He tried to read a novel. Finally he phoned Hank Brown—the Special Agent working on the Flesher case.

"Hello, Hank, this is Jeff Burke. What's new?"

"Not much. Same old stuff. Did you hear about the revenue agent in the Washington office—Rod Taylor, I believe? He was convicted of filing false returns and using the mail to defraud the government ... a thirteen-count indictment."

"You mean he didn't file his own tax returns? How stupid."

"No, no. It's more involved than that. Apparently, he obtained the names of eight taxpayers and filed fraudulent income tax returns in their names. He even sent in W-2 withholding forms showing them working for Acme Industries."

"Very original company," smiled Jeff. "That's what prisoners do in prisons."

"Anyway, the returns each claimed partnership losses sufficient to entitle the taxpayer a refund ranging from $12,000 to $16,000.

The fake returns gave false addresses to rooming houses and transient hotels where rooms had been rented in the taxpayers' names."

"How did the agent get the money?" asked Jeff.

"The revenue agent had his brother and another accomplice working with him on the scheme. The refund checks were picked up by his brother and deposited in bank accounts opened in the taxpayers' names at four banks. Later the money was withdrawn."

"How did they catch the agent?"

"I don't know. Maybe an informant. But the accomplice testified against him in court. And they used the agent's own tax return against him."

"How?"

"Man, don't ask so many questions. I'll tell you the whole story. Your suspension has got you up a tree, huh?"

Jeff didn't respond.

Hank continued. "His handwriting on the bodies of the tax returns was used as examples of his handwriting and gave the experts a chance to say that the fake returns were prepared by the agent. Apparently, he wrote all of the tax returns in block capitals like on his H.R. or personnel forms."

"He was a dummy," Jeff responded. "Why didn't the agent argue that the admission of his tax return into evidence was prohibited by the confidentiality provisions?"

"He did argue that, but lost. Why did you call?"

"Oh, just to catch up on the Flesher case. What's happening?"

"Not much," replied Hank. "We have not been able to touch B.W. We did find out that he has an interest in a rare coin shop."

"Which one?" Jeff almost shouted.

"A Rosenbaum shop in the northeast section. Why?"

"This Rosenbaum shop is a member of a chain of about 1,500 rare coin and stamp stores all over the U.S. I believe they are not only paying no taxes, but each store is ripping off refunds of about $150,000 each year. If organized crime is into the action…"

"Wow. Double wow!" exclaimed Hank. "How?"

"Don't ask so many questions," Jeff mocked, followed by a controlled chuckle.

"Cut the crap, Jeff."

"Okay, okay. Each shop indicates to the regional offices that they are filing a separate return and each obtains a refund. The headquarters in Phoenix is filing a consolidated return and offsets all of these 1,500 net operating losses against the parent company's income."

"Pretty good," replied Hank. "Why aren't they caught?"

"I'll tell you if you will let me work with you. I'll stake out the coin shop B.W. owns,"

"I don't know. You're trouble."

"Come on."

"You'll have to do it on your own. I'll keep you informed. But I'll deny having anything to do with you if there's trouble. Is that satisfactory?"

"Fine. There's a computer fellow in Martinsburg who is covering up the fraud."

"Have you reported him to TIGTA?" TIGTA refers to the Treasury Inspector General for Tax Administration. TIGTA provides independent oversight of IRS activities. They are committed to the prevention and detection of fraud, waste, and abuse within the IRS.

"Yes. I'm working closely with Jason Pabst. He was Nick Anderson's supervisor before Nick was killed by the model plane explosion. I believe his killing is involved with the Onner affair."

"Please stay away from me! I am too young to die."

"What connection does B.W. have with the rare coin shop?" Jeff asked.

"B.W. only owns 30% of the coin shop, but he actually does much of the buying. He's a coin freak. A numismatist, I believe they are called."

"Do you think they are using the shop to launder their illegal profits?" asked Jeff.

"Could be. I hadn't thought about that. Do you know what B.W. looks like?"

"Yes, I've seen photos of him. I'll start watching him today. Here's an idea. Could you get your supervisor to furnish you with an estate made up of rare coins — say 20? I could sell the estate to the coin shop, and we could follow the coins through their accounting system to see if they are laundering money."

"I don't know. He wants to catch B.W. for sure. Let me check with him. I'll call you tonight."

Jeff immediately called Jason Pabst and told him about the possible organized crime connection with the Rosenbaum coin company.

"I'm going to start shadowing B.W. Flesher this afternoon," Jeff told Jason.

"Be careful," was all that Jason said.

The Rosenbaum Coin and Stamp shop was in a large shopping center off the freeway. The shop was small, but located near heavy walking traffic.

Jeff went up to the entrance, but the door was locked. A sign indicated to ring the bell. Jeff punched the bell with his index finger. A short, sandy-haired man in his mid-thirties looked up and pushed a lever behind a counter which unlocked the door.

"Hi there," was the friendly response from the handsome man behind the counter.

"Are you afraid someone is going to get in?" joked Jeff.

"Actually, it's there to slow anyone down who wants to get out. I won't let you out until you buy something," laughed the man. "Can I help you?"

"Well, I would like to sell some coins."

"Good, we buy coins, too. Did you bring them?"

"No, my father died several months ago and left them to me. I have them in my safe deposit box."

"I'm sorry about your father. I'll have to get Mr. Flesher to look at the coins. He does most of our buying. Could you give me your name and telephone number? He'll set up an appointment and meet you at the safe deposit box."

"I'll be out of town the next several days. Can I call him instead?"

"Sure. Here's his card. His office and home telephone numbers are listed. What is your name?"

"Burke. May I look around?"

"Help yourself. Do you know anything about coins?" asked the young man.

"Not really," replied Jeff as he strolled around the small shop. It was quite similar to the Rosenbaum shop in Martinsburg. Finally he walked over to the door to get out. He couldn't — it was locked.

The young man looked at Jeff and smiled. "You haven't bought anything yet." He reached down behind the counter and pushed a button. Jeff walked out. He mentally jotted down a notice that he had seen on the small bulletin board: Important Coin Show, Sheraton Convention Center, Lanham, Maryland, 7:30. Two weeks from then.

That evening Hank called.

"We're in luck. My boss will get a coin collection — about 20 coins. But you'll have to sell them close to the cost value to the department. Where do you bank? Do you have a safe deposit box?"

"Municipal Bank & Trust. No box. I don't have anything to save. But I'll get one tomorrow."

"Then call me after lunch tomorrow, and I'll bring the coins to your bank. We're going out on the limb working with you. Don't mess up. My bosses don't know this might involve the Onner affair. So keep your mouth shut. We'll have accurate descriptions of each of the coins. Should I mark each coin with an anthracene pencil?"

Jeff thought for a moment. "Yes, put your initials on the coins. Surely they don't check all the coins they buy. Will your boss pay for the safe deposit box?"

"Good grief, Burke. Save your receipt. See you tomorrow. Don't take any wooden nickels." Hank was laughing loudly as he hung up the phone.

Jeff was up early the next morning. He was at the public library when the doors opened, and he checked out five books on coin collecting.

Back at his apartment he began reading. He made only three calls during the day. One was to his bank to reserve a small bank deposit box. The second one was to B.W. Flesher to set up an appointment at 2:00 the next afternoon in order for him to appraise the rare coins — he used the name Burke Jefferies. The third call was to Hank. He met Hank at the Municipal Bank where they deposited the rare coins in his bank deposit box. Their total wholesale value was approximately $18,500.

That evening and the next morning, Jeff continued to read about coin collecting. He read how coins are minted from a master die. He read about silver dollars, commemorative coins, trade dollars, Eagle gold coins, $3 gold pieces, type coins, half cents, large cents, half dimes, Liberty Seated half dollar, coin rolls, the *Red Book,* 1917 Matte Proof Nickel, proof sets, the Charlotte mint, and much more.

He read about the end of inflation in Germany in 1923. After seven years of constantly accelerating inflation, the German mark finally stabilized at the rate of four trillion, two billion (4,002,000,000,000) to one U.S. gold dollar. Jeff knew that the U.S. dollar was no longer backed by gold. With a $18 trillion debt, inflation had to rear its ugly head soon. The federal government only collected about $2.3 trillion each year.

Jeff was at the bank early. He made arrangements to get to his safe deposit box and waited for B.W. Flesher to arrive.

B.W. was a husky, well-dressed man with the build of a highly trained athlete. He did not fit the stereotype image of an organized crime member. Of course, they never do. Jeff recognized B.W. Flesher when he entered the bank.

Jeff walked over and introduced himself. "Hello, Mr. Flesher. I'm Burke Jefferies. I'm glad you could come."

"Oh, I'm always happy to look at rare coins, my son. I'm sorry I am late. Got behind some slow traffic. What do you have for me?"

"There are about 20 coins. I'm not exactly sure what I have. As I mentioned on the phone, my father left them to me."

"There is nothing better than the inheritance of rare coins. Sorry about your father."

Jeff and Mr. Flesher followed a pretty, redheaded bank employee into the vault. She wore a tight skirt and a loose, light blue blouse. She smiled as she opened the box and said in a sweet voice, "Call me when you are finished gentlemen."

Jeff carried the metal box over to a small room for privacy. They had to leave the door open slightly because the room was not big enough for two people.

"By the way, Mr. Jefferies, my name is Wayne. May I call you Burke?"

"Yes, please do."

B.W.'s eyes seemed to glitter as he saw the coins in the box as Jeff opened it. B.W. picked up the first coin and looked at it closely. "Your father was a connoisseur. Most of these are gold coins. The Arabs continue to trade their billions of dollars of oil for gold. They understand inflation. Did you know that the Germans took the entire nation of Italy out of hock for gold?"

B.W. didn't wait for the response to his question. "Are you a numismatist?"

"Not really. I know a little about coins."

"See this five dollar half edge? A draped bust left. Magnificent! An 1809 over 8." B.W. was carefully holding the coin on its edges for Jeff to see. He was really talking to himself, not Jeff.

"Notice the 8 within the 9. Here, look through the glass. Can you see the 8?"

"Yes. Is that good or bad? Is a defective coin worth more or less?"

"Worth much more, my young man. The denticles on the obverse in the area above Miss Liberty are practically nonexistent."

B.W. picked up another coin. "An 1849 $10 eagle, no motto. Only about 650 of these coins were minted," B.W. did not look at Jeff as he talked.

"Here's a double eagle 1879-O twenty dollar piece. The 'O' mint-mark means that it was minted in New Orleans. It's the only New Orleans mint double eagle with motto. Breathtaking!"

B.W. took out a pad of paper from his brown leather briefcase and began to write down a list of the coins and their conditions. After making the inventory, he took out a gray looking newsletter and began to look for prices.

"Are those gray sheets?" Jeff asked.

"Why, yes." B.W. looked a little confused. "I thought you knew little about coins?"

Jeff didn't respond. He knew that the "gray sheets" gave the wholesale price of the coins — both a "bid" and an "ask" price. Somewhat like over-the-counter stock.

Jeff watched as B.W. marked prices for each coin which he had listed. Finally B.W. looked up and said, "You are a very lucky young man. There are several very good coins here. But some of the coins are in poor condition. I'm willing to offer you $16,250 for all of them. Notice that I'll take the ones in poor condition from you also."

Jeff paused as if he were thinking about the offer. Then he said, "Mr. Flesher, another dealer has offered me $17,750."

"Call me Wayne, please," B.W. said softly. "Gold is the instrument of gamblers and speculators, and the idol of the miser and the thief."

"What?" was Jeff's puzzled response.

"Just an old saying, Burke. You know, of course, that gold is the metal that men dig out of holes for dentists and governments to put back in." B.W. paused and then continued. "I'm merely joking. What is your occupation?"

"I'm a bookkeeper," Jeff lied.

"Really, I just lost my bookkeeper. Who do you work for?"

"No one really. I'm an independent contractor. I do jobs for a number of clients."

"Are you good?"

"I believe so."

"It's much better to have your gold in the hand than in the heart. I'll give you $17,900 for the coins. Can you get me some references? I need to hire a part-time bookkeeper."

Jeff smiled. "It's a sale — for the first question. And yes, I can get you references with respect to the second question."

"Good, then it's a deal." B.W. stuck out his hand and Jeff shook it. B.W's grip was very muscular. "Will you accept one half of the amount by check and the other half in cash?"

"Will the check bounce?"

"No."

"Are you going to carry the coins out now?"

B.W. patted under his left shoulder. "I have a weapon." B.W. wrote the check and then counted out 89 $100 bills. He then put the coins in his briefcase. "The receipt of cash can help you out taxwise. Do you understand?" Jeff shook his head. "Don't forget to call and give me some references."

Jeff later watched as B.W. drove off in his light blue Lincoln Continental. He then opened up a bank account with the $8,900 cash and the $9,000 Rosenbaum check.

One hour later Jeff called Hank. "Hey, Hank, I made the coin collection sale for $17,900."

"What? That's below wholesale value," moaned Hank.

"But that's not all. I can get a part-time job working on his books. He needs a bookkeeper," Jeff replied.

"You can't add 12 and 12. But, on the bright side, your paychecks can be used to make up the difference you lost on the coins."

"Can we line up some references for me? I told B.W. — uh, Wayne—that I was an independent contractor. I used the name Burke Jefferies. Today it is more difficult for IRS employees to use pseudonyms. Adequate justification for the use must be provided by the employee, and its use must be approved by the employee's supervisor. Do you think you can handle this approval?" Jeff asked politely.

"That's an original name, for sure. I'll get you a social security number under that name. That's easier than trying to find three people who would recommend you even for dogcatcher. Do you even know how to keep books?" Hank was serious.

"I'm offended. Old accountants never die, they just lose their balance. I got a degree in accounting from Penn State."

"Is that in the United States?" Hank asked.

"Get back to work," Jeff responded. "Penn State always has a good football team."

"Not better than Alabama," Hank said.

"Even LSU beat Alabama this year."

Chapter 21

Another difference between death and taxes is that death
is frequently painless.

—Anonymous

For the next several weeks Jeff Burke (using the name Burke Jefferies) spent a number of hours on the books and records of Rosenbaum Coin and Stamp Shop. Jeff was able to work with B.W., who
managed to drop by the shop daily.

Jeff reported regularly to Hank as to what he observed, heard,
and read in the coin shop. He had free access to the entire shop —
it wasn't large. He read materials on or in the desks and elsewhere
in the shop. He asked questions of the other employees as to how
the business was conducted.

From the young man whom Jeff had talked to during his first
visit to the coin shop, Jeff learned that although the Rosenbaum
Company owned seventy percent of the shop, B.W. Flesher exerted
much power for a 30% owner.

While posting the financial transactions and watching the flow
of money, Jeff found out how B.W. was laundering his illegal profits through the coin shop. B.W. did almost all of the buying of the
rare coins.

B.W. was understating most purchases. For example, of the
$17,900 purchase from Jeff, only $9,000 came through the coin
shop. Jeff reasoned that the $8,900 difference came from cash from
B.W.'s other illegal businesses.

Understatement of purchases, of course, overstated the final income figure of the coin shop. But since the coin shop was paying
no taxes because of the computer manipulation of Richard Onner,

"dirty money" was turned into "clean money" in a "legit" coin business. Onner was overriding the cross checks between parent and subsidiary tax returns.

During the second week of undercover employment, Jeff talked B.W. into taking him to the Lanham Coin Show. Jeff met B.W. at the Sheraton Convention Center in Lanham, Maryland, around 10:00 Wednesday morning.

"Hello, Burke. Did you have any trouble finding the place?"

"No, not really."

"Suppose we go to the bourse area first. The auction starts at 12:30. You stick close to me, and you can learn something about coins."

In the bourse area there were approximately 300 eight-foot bourse tables. Behind each table was a dealer in either coins, stamps, silver, gold, and other collectibles — or some combination. The coin show was a large one.

Jeff was amazed as B.W. effectively went from one table to the next looking for something to buy. He bought a draped bust 1801 half dollar (Type III) at one table, and a brilliant uncirculated 1856 flying eagle small cent from another dealer after he argued convincingly that the coin was a slider (e.g., not really uncirculated).

For most of the coins, B.W. paid cash. Occasionally, he would write a Rosenbaum check for a particular coin. For the more expensive coins he normally paid cash. At one table he paid 20 one hundred-dollar bills for an 1874-S, MS-60, $20 Liberty Gold piece. B.W. told Jeff that the S mintmark stood for San Francisco.

At another table he gave 17 $100 bills for a 1934-S, MS-60, Peace dollar. Here, as in most situations, B.W. was able to get the dealer to reduce his selling price by $500.

By 12:20 they had covered only about 100 tables. Jeff had noticed dealers such as New England Rare Coin Galleries, New World Rarities, Pinnacle Rarities, J.I. Teaparty, Royal Enterprises, Modern Coin Mart, Carolina Coins & Stamp, Paramount International, Deep South Rare Coins, American Rarities, Nevada Coin Mart, Kagin's, Freemont Coins, Bower & Merena, and other "blue chip" coin dealers.

At one table Jeff almost bought a "Hide It." This item was a secret book safe. It looked just like any real book, but opened to reveal a combination lock safe. Jeff thought it was big enough to hold
all of the bribes he had accepted — exactly zero. But B.W. tapped
him on the shoulder and said, "Let's get a coke and hot dog and go
to the auction."

The auction was the "Breen IX Auction Sale" presented by the Oak
Tree Auction Galleries. The pamphlet explaining the sale indicated
that there were more than 1,600 lots. It seemed that B.W. bid on
many of them, from Colonial coins, U.S. Type coins, Morgan silver dollars, Peace dollars (Jeff wondered if this should have been
spelled Piece), gold coins, to mint sets.

B.W. certainly knew how to handle himself at the auction. The
auctioneer apparently knew B.W. because he only had to move his
pencil to bid. Jeff could not always follow the bidding, but B.W.
seemed to know exactly what was happening. The auctioneer talked
too fast for Jeff. He seemed to have a rapid, dry drawl of someone
from the Southwest.

Around 4:00 p.m. Jeff whispered to B.W., "I'm going outside to
get something to eat. My tail is getting tired."

B.W. waved him out. "Go on and see the exhibits. Only a coina-
holic could sit in here all afternoon." He was deeply engrossed in the
next coin up for bid. Outside the auction room, Jeff reached down
and picked up a brochure from an exhibit. It was an old invitation
to join the Society of Bearded Numismatists (SOB). Someone was
trying to restart the society.

After glancing at the humorous poem entitled "On Being Invited
to join S.O.B. Numismatists," Jeff turned the brochure over and
began to jot down as many of the purchases that B.W. had made in
the bourse area and during the auction as he could recall. He was
able to list 12 with prices and 16 more without prices. The books which
he had read in the past several weeks on rare coins had helped him
to recall a reasonable description of the coin purchases.

Jeff bought some light beer and another hot dog. He started
watching a slide-illustrated program on the "History of the Philip-
pines' Money and the Japanese Occupational Notes." He left before

it was over. Next he glanced at a 10-panel exhibit of the coinage of the world from ancient to modern times.

As he was perusing the crowd, unconsciously looking for the blonde head of Debra Sweeney, B.W. came up and tapped him on the shoulder. "Can you follow me to my home? I have a small fortune in this briefcase. I have a safe at home."

"Be glad to."

"Do you want to attend the auction tomorrow morning?"

"Yes, if you don't mind. I'm really getting interested in coins."

"Okay."

Jeff followed B.W. to his home in the northeast of Baltimore. It was a modest home with a swimming pool. But there was also a tennis court. Still, the house did look incongruous with a light blue Lincoln and a light tan Cadillac sitting in front of it.

Jeff was not invited into B.W.'s house.

The next day Jeff sat through the entire auction with B.W. He later watched B.W. pay for the coins with more one hundred dollar bills. Afterward, Jeff recorded for future reference 16 items with prices and 12 coins without prices which B.W. had purchased at the auction. He had purchased many high-priced coins.

During the next several days following the auction, B.W. brought most of the rare coins into the inventory of the coin shop. They were recorded on the books at low purchase prices. The coins were then sold at reasonable prices to investors and dealers (including many to the other Rosenbaum shops).

Late Thursday Jeff called Hank Brown from his apartment. "Hank, I believe I have about as much evidence as I am going to get on B.W. The longer I hang around, the higher the odds are that someone is going to recognize me. I believe we should do our thing."

"Can you make photocopies of his books and records?" asked Hank.

"I doubt it. There's always someone around. It would be too risky taking the records out of the store at night to be copied. Once they suspect something they'll destroy the books."

"Could you use a camera?"

"Not really. Someone would see me for sure."

"So we are going to have to seize his books and records," Hank concluded.

"Probably. I don't know any other way. I'll try to get some shots with my cell phone."

"Could you prepare an affidavit tonight with the information you have gathered? We'll take it to a magistrate tomorrow morning at 10:30 and get a search warrant. We can hit Flesher's coin shop in the afternoon."

"It's Rosenbaum Coins and Stamps," Jeff interjected.

"Sure, sure. See you at 10:30."

Jeff's affidavit was convincing, and the magistrate provided a search warrant.

The short, sandy-haired employee, Hesse, looked up when Jeff rang the buzzer. He automatically pushed the button and Hank Brown followed Jeff into the small shop.

"B.W. is in the back, Burke," Hesse advised.

"Hesse, this is Special Agent Hank Brown. I'm also a Special Agent, Jeff Burke."

Hank handed the young man the search warrant and said, "We would like to see all of the books and records that are here."

The employee was shocked. He slowly read the front part of the search warrant. Finally he turned and shouted, "Mr. Flesher, you better come out here."

B.W. walked out, smiled, and said, "I wasn't expecting you today, Burke."

"Mr. Flesher, he's.... he's an IRS agent."

For a moment B.W. didn't move. He merely shot an angry, gunmetal stare at Jeff. He regained some composure and said, "How can I help you gentlemen?"

The employee gave the search warrant to B.W., who read it slowly. He looked up at Jeff and said, "You creep." He waved his arm and sat down in a chair. "Hesse, call my lawyer and tell him to get over here fast." Turning to Hank, he said, "Please wait until my lawyer gets here."

"I'm sorry, Mr. Flesher, there is no need for a lawyer. Where are your books and records?" Hank asked.

"Burke knows where they are," shot back B.W., "or whatever his name is."

"My real name is Jeff Burke, Mr. Flesher."

B.W. Flesher did not respond. He was tired. He didn't know what to do.

Hank and Jeff made a thorough search of the entire coin shop. They seized all of the books and records, over the angry objections of B.W. Flesher.

Two days later Hank called Jeff.

"Flesher has had his lawyers working overtime. He has filed an action seeking money damages, the return of his books, and records, and an injunction on the use of his documents in any future criminal proceedings."

"What money damages?" asked Jeff.

"He maintains we violated his Fourth Amendment rights. Plus he wants compensation for his books and records."

"Fine. Make copies of his real books and records and give them back to him. That'll do away with any real monetary damages. He might get some nominal damages for the invasion of his privacy. But will he not go to jail? He can use the nominal damages to buy cigarettes. What about the injunction?"

"Our lawyers believe the injunction is premature. If we bring a civil tax suit against him, there's no problem. Such an injunction in a civil action is a premature claim. In a future criminal proceeding against him, the injunction may be proper."

"So do our lawyers think we have him?" asked Jeff.

"They believe so. You did a good job."

"Don't forget to send me the reimbursement for the bank deposit box."

"You'll be lucky if you are not locked up with Flesher. Good luck on the outcome of your suspension. If there is any way I can help, seriously, give me a call."

* * *

"Hello, is this Box 20011?"

"Yes," was the crisp response.

"The additional money is in your account. You must terminate the two parties within 48 hours. Why is it taking you so long on the first party?" The male caller was clearly disturbed.

"Just problems, that's all. It will be done." Click.

* * *

Later that night Jeff received an important phone call from Rick Garrison.

"Jeff, this is Rick Garrison. Debra Sweeney is on the move again. She contacted someone in Washington on the pay telephone. I taped her conversation. She received new instructions. She must kill you within 48 hours along with someone named Jason Pabst," continued Garrison in a very rapid voice.

"Figures. Pabst is the internal security inspector working with me. Her contact really has an almost instantaneous information flow. Who could it be?" asked Jeff almost to himself.

"We are at the airport now. She is catching a plane to Washington in about twenty minutes. Call this Pabst fellow and let him know the danger. I'm going to follow her."

Jeff tried until he fell asleep to call Jason Pabst. He had no success. He had placed a chair against his doorknob. His bedfellow that night was a .38 revolver within easy reach. Washington was only a short flight from Baltimore.

The ringing in his ears made him jump. It was only the phone. The glow of his clock indicated that it was only 6:14 a.m.

"Hello," mumbled Jeff.

"I lost her," shouted Garrison into the phone. "I lost her cab when she drove into Washington. Did you contact Pabst?"

"No, I couldn't get him on the phone. No one would answer."

"Debra's contact gave her his address. I'll try to beat her there."

"Did you recognize her contact?"

"No, it was a male caller. Keep calling Pabst."

Jeff dialed Pabst's number. There was no answer. He dialed information to check to make sure he had the right number. He did, and called again several times. There was no answer.

Chapter 22

Collecting more taxes than is absolutely necessary is legalized robbery.

—Calvin Coolidge

Debra Sweeney was in a distressed mood. She had attempted to eliminate Jeff Burke three times. She had failed three times. Why had he not drunk the coffee and eaten the Danish she left for him at the Hilton? The poison would have killed him in three minutes.

Her contact in Washington had given her a time limitation. She did not like to work under a deadline. There was more chance of a fatal mistake. But on the bright side, the extra assignment meant a larger payoff.

She did not know who had hired her. The first contact had been by a typed letter with instructions to her code-name mail box in Elkhorn City. Her mother still lived there. She could vividly remember her abused early childhood. After the initial contact she had used a pay telephone, calling a pay telephone at a certain time in Washington, D.C.

Debra had gotten into her financially rewarding business by accident. When her husband had a church in Ashland, Kentucky, she had hit a man walking along the side of the road with her car late in the evening. She had panicked and left the scene of the accident. Although the man died, she was never caught.

Her older child was beginning his freshman year at Princeton. A minister's salary simply was not enough to pay the tuition. But they were not poor enough for her son to receive financial support from the University. One evening she was watching a movie about a "hit woman." Almost as a joke she sent a short advertisement to an underground Los Angeles newspaper:

> Very personal extermination service. Quick and inexpensive. Write Box 20011, Elkhorn, KY. Send pay phone number and a specific time when you can be called.

The ad ran for four weeks. During the third week she received a response. She called the respondent who apparently wanted a labor union official eliminated. She stalled, indicating that she had already accepted too many jobs. However, she made arrangements to call the respondent in three weeks.

She established a bank account in Lausanne, Switzerland. When she returned the call, she instructed the male caller to deposit ten thousand dollars in her numbered account. She told him to send a photograph of the intended victim along with pertinent data.

When the money was deposited, Debra intended to keep the money and forget about the hit. But she flew to San Diego for an Aeronautics Convention. She drove to Long Beach, and followed the union official for about two days. She shot the man at point blank range with a pistol. The Los Angeles papers indicated that the assassination was part of a gangland war.

Each subsequent hit became easier and easier. Her trademark was to vary the manner of terminating the victim to confuse the authorities. She had not advertised for several years. As she became more efficient, word of mouth advertising brought in enough work to send two children to expensive universities. She now had a Swiss bank account of about $690,000.

To disguise the source of income from her husband, Debra began writing children's books. Since she handled the finances in her family, it was fairly easy to report to her husband that she had received a "fat" royalty check from her publisher. Her husband was continually encouraging her to write more books. He was especially proud of the ten-percent tithe which she gave to the church from her "royalties."

Debra had flown to Washington and taken a taxi to a nondescript motel. She did not want to rush her work. Fewer mistakes were made when a contract was planned carefully.

A slight tinge of excitement raced through her body as she worked in her motel room that night. She had a special termination technique for Jason Pabst. She had an extract from the tree *Unonopsis veneficiorum* that grew in the upper Amazon region. Indian tribes used this poison to tip their blowgun darts and arrows.

This compound into which she was dipping the small dart would prevent nerve impulses from activating skeletal and voluntary muscles. An injection would first affect the muscles of the ears, eyes and toes, then those of the limbs and neck, and finally the respiratory muscles. Respiratory paralysis would eventually cause a painless death.

As for Jeff Burke—the man with three lives—she had a special exotic death planned.

Ironically, on the nightstand next to the telephone was a Gideon Bible. Someone had left the Bible open to Chapter 10 of Matthew. Verse 26 had been underlined.

> There is nothing covered that shall not be revealed; and hid that shall not be known.

In her navy-tailored suit, white blouse, brown wig, and wide-rimmed glasses, Debra was watching Jason Pabst emerge from his apartment house. A tall gentleman in his mid-thirties was with Mr. Pabst. The man seemed vaguely familiar to Debra.

Although both men seemed to be glancing from side to side, they did not see Debra in her car. It was very cold. She followed them to a subway station. She got on the same subway, but in a different car. When they emerged from the underground subway near Constitution Avenue, she followed at a safe distance. They walked toward the IRS building.

About one block from their destination, she walked up rapidly behind them as they stopped at a crosswalk. There were about eight people waiting at the crosswalk. She removed her mirror and the blowgun from her purse. While pretending to put on lipstick, she aimed the long lipstick tube at Jason's neck. She blew the poisonous dart. Rather than hitting his neck, the dart hit his left shoulder blade.

Debra turned right and walked away as the "walk" light began blinking. She knew that the dart had probably penetrated his overcoat. Time would complete this half of her contract. Surprisingly, Jason Pabst was still walking as he entered 1111 Constitution Avenue. His overcoat may have slowed the effect of the poison.

Rick Garrison and Jason Pabst walked to Jason's office on the third floor.

"She didn't get me this morning," said Jason as he walked over to his coat rack. He wiped several small beads of sweat from his forehead.

"Just a second, there's a bug or something on your coat," commanded Rick. He walked over and pulled something from Jason's coat. "It's a dart! Have your children been using your coat as a dart board?"

"We don't have any darts," replied Jason.

"Wait a minute. Maybe she did get to you. This could be a poison dart. The strap on your bullet-proof vest must have kept the point from reaching your body."

"Here, put that thing in this envelope, and we'll have it analyzed by the Intelligence Division. We have got to find her. Am I glad you talked me into wearing this vest," responded Jason as he shook his head slowly.

"You know what we should do? She had instructions to kill you within 48 hours. Someone important wants you rubbed out. Why don't I call an ambulance, and take you to the hospital? We can then shadow Burke and try to get her before she kills him."

"I don't know," replied Jason.

"Look, I feel responsible. I should have arrested her in Pikeville. If she knocks both of you off, how do you think I'm going to feel? Call your wife and let her know what is happening. We can call Burke and warn him. We need to let him know what has transpired."

"Okay, if you insist."

When the ambulance arrived at the front of the IRS building, two attendants hurried to the third floor and carried Jason back to the waiting vehicle. A small crowd watched the ambulance move down Constitution Avenue with its siren screaming.

Once the ambulance disappeared, Debra walked down the street and caught a taxi to the airport.

In the late evening newspaper, there was a small notice on page 25:

Jason Pabst, an Internal Revenue Service Agent, died today on arrival at St. Mary's Hospital. Cause of death is unknown. Funeral arrangements are pending.

Jeff had waited in his apartment until Jason Pabst had arrived. After the staged ride in the ambulance, Jason and Rick had driven to Jeff's apartment in Baltimore.

The plan was for Garrison to stay with Jeff. Jason was to follow at a safe distance in the hopes of observing Debra Sweeney following Jeff. Jason looked ridiculous in sunglasses and an Orioles baseball hat.

After some discussion, Jeff and Garrison left in order to drive to Jeff's office. Upon leaving his apartment, Jeff placed a small piece of transparent tape on the top of his door attached to the doorframe. If Debra came into his apartment, she would disturb the tape.

When he parked his car in Baltimore, Jeff took the same precautions. He locked both doors and placed a small piece of transparent tape at the bottom of each door, attached to the frame of the car.

Once at his office, Jeff picked up the photographs he had taken in Phoenix. He was spreading them out on his desk showing them to Rick when Jason entered his office.

"Well, did you see her following us?" inquired Jeff, looking up from the pictures.

"Nope, not a glimpse," replied Jason. He had already removed the sunglasses and baseball hat. He walked over and looked at the photos.

"Hmm, interesting," said Jason as he scratched his forehead. "Would you believe that your mysterious conspirator looks somewhat like Commissioner Callaway. Mind you, not much evidence because of the straw hat and glasses, but if it is Jimmy Callaway, that would explain why you were relieved of duty for two weeks. We may have found a big can of snakes. I probably have a termination notice back at my office."

"I thought he looked familiar," exclaimed Jeff. "I just couldn't place his face."

Jason turned to Jeff. "Did you get a list of the telephone calls made to and from the pay phone that Debra used?"

"No, I never got around to it," replied Jeff.

"Can I use your phone, Jeff?" asked Jason. "I'll call and have those phone numbers sent to you."

"Sure. Dial nine to get outside."

Both Jeff and Rick sat down while Jason made arrangements for the telephone numbers to be faxed to Jeff's home address.

When Jason hung up, Jeff spoke to him. "How much power do you have? We are in big trouble if Callaway is involved."

"Theoretically, I'm supposed to report directly to the Commissioner. Under the circumstances I probably should report the matter to Secretary of the Treasury Clyde Hickey. To protect us I should sit down and type a short letter to the Secretary, explaining our suspicions. Let me type a letter on your computer."

"Sure." Jeff pointed to his computer.

After Jason left, Jeff turned to Rick. "What do we do now?"

"Beats me!"

"If we can't find Debra, we probably should get Onner. He's the computer employee at Martinsburg who is helping the Rosenbaum Company obtain about $225 million of illegal tax refunds each year."

"Forget about finding Debra. She'll find you," said Rick. "You better hope we see her first. I wonder how and when she is going to try to kill you?"

Jeff sat silent for several minutes. He wondered if it was worth the trouble of being a Special Agent. He could always take a safe job such as a barber or an accountant. He could probably make more money, too. He had never heard of a barber or an account-ant being shot by a professional killer. But as "deep pockets," accountants were being sued more frequently.

Jason interrupted Jeff's thoughts as he entered the office. "Here, how does it sound?" Jason handed both Jeff and Rick a copy of the letter he had typed. "I'm going to send Attorney General Ben Gibson a copy since the Justice Department will eventually have to prosecute."

> Honorable Clyde Hickey
> Secretary of the Treasury
> 1111 Constitution Avenue
> Washington, D.C. 20013
>
> Dear Mr. Hickey:
>
> I am a member of the Internal Security Office which investigates corruption within the IRS. Special Agent Jeff Burke (Baltimore) and Detective Rick Garrison (Washington, D.C.), and I believe that Commissioner Jimmy Callaway may be involved with Richard Onner (IRS computer employee—Martinsburg, WV) and other unknown parties in a massive fraud within the IRS.
>
> The fraud involves approximately 1,500 coin shops controlled by Rosenbaum Company (headquarters in Phoenix, Arizona). One of my special strike force agents (Nick Anderson) has already been killed, apparently by Debra Sweeney (Pikeville, KY), a professional killer. Sweeney also has made an attempt on my life. I staged my death and am now working closely with Jeff Burke. Detective Garrison intercepted a telephone message from an unknown individual to Debra Sweeney with instructions to kill Jeff Burke and myself within 48 hours.

An individual who appears to be Commissioner Callaway met with Jack Rosenbaum and Tony Blake (Phoenix IRS agent) in the Pepper Tree establishment in Phoenix approximately two weeks ago. Enclosed is a photo of this meeting. Other photos and negatives may be obtained from Jeff Burke.

Due to the sensitive nature of this matter, only yourself, Jeff Burke, Rick Garrison, and Attorney General Gibson have received copies of this letter.

Sincerely,

Jason Pabst
Group Supervisor
"Clean House" Strike Force
Jp:jp
cc: Attorney General Ben Gibson, Jeff Burke, Rick Garrison.

"Looks good to me," said Jeff.

"Same here," agreed Rick, handing the copy of the letter back to Jason.

"Both of you keep a copy of the letter. I'll keep a copy and mail the original to the Secretary today."

After Jeff filed away his copy, Jason spoke to him. "If you are going to be our guinea pig, we should leave for your apartment. If we avoid the rush on the streets, we should have a better chance of spotting Debra. Rick, you stick on him like a flea. I'll follow close behind." Jason put on his sunglasses, his ridiculous baseball hat and overcoat, and walked out the door first.

Chapter 23

American workers spend more of their day working to pay taxes than they do to feed, clothe, and house their families.

—The Tax Foundation

There are seven species of the Genus Naja: the cobra. A cobra is quick and agile. When annoyed or frightened, a cobra rears and spreads his hood as a warning. A cobra can strike with rapidity and has a tendency to hold on after biting a victim.

The Cape cobra, *Naia Nivea*, is found in the Cape Province and certain areas of Southwestern Africa. It is probably the most dangerous of all cobras. The Cape cobra is courageous and will face its foe. Its potent venom will cause death within a few hours. Its bite can kill a 6,000-pound elephant. Less than two drops of *Naia Nivea* venom is sufficient to kill an average sized man. This cobra can produce 15 drops with ease. This poison is so deadly that the only thing you can do if you've been bitten is die.

* * *

Jeff's walk to his auto was uneventful. Jeff and Rick saw Jason drop his letters to the Secretary of the Treasury and the Attorney General in a mailbox. Before Jeff and Rick got into the car, they checked the transparent tape on both doors. The tape had not been disturbed. Before entering his apartment, Jeff checked and saw that the transparent tape on his door had not been disturbed. Jason parked some distance from Jeff's apartment and waited about thirty minutes before he knocked and entered.

That evening they decided to go to the Justice Department the next morning to make arrangements for arresting Richard Onner.

They also needed to start action against the Rosenbaum Company. They did not know what to do about the Commissioner. Maybe Onner or Jack Rosenbaum would implicate Commissioner Callaway.

Early in the morning Debra Sweeney placed a reed basket on the ground near a car. Within a minute she was able to open the door on the driver's side. She put on some work gloves. Gingerly she removed the top from the basket and shook a four-foot long cobra on the back floor of the dirty automobile. With a long curved rod she was able to force the snake under the front seat. The alarming hiss and flaring hood of the cobra would bring a taste of fear even to a hardened criminal. Another minute fled by and Debra locked the door, carefully replaced the tape on the door, and disappeared.

Around seven-thirty Jeff awoke from his dreams. He went into his kitchen, removed a box of Raisin Bran from a cabinet and a gallon of milk from his refrigerator. His movements awoke Rick and Jason, who came into the kitchen to eat.

"Do you have any Pop Tarts?" asked Jason.

"No, cereal is all I have," replied Jeff. "I do have some orange juice."

They ate in silence.

Jason was the first to leave. He left by the back door. He went around to the front of the apartment wearing his sunglasses and the Orioles' hat. Nothing appeared to be out of the ordinary. Jason unlocked his car door and got in so that he could be able to watch when Jeff and Rick left. Jason had not left any transparent tape on his car doors.

Rick was the first to come out of the apartment door. He looked around and then motioned for Jeff to come out. Jeff locked his door and placed some more tape at the top of his front door.

Once at his car, Jeff checked both doors. The tape was still there. After unlocking the doors, Jeff and Rick got into the car.

Jeff drove through the parking lot and stopped at the entrance. He glanced in the rear view mirror and saw Jason driving up behind him.

"Hey, what do you have in your car?" shouted Rick. His left leg jerked forward, and he reached down and slapped at his leg. The sharp pain stopped in his leg, but something bit him on his left hand. "Damn!" bellowed Rick.

Jeff looked over at Rick. A snake was holding on to Rick's hand. The sight of the snake made his flesh crawl.

Rick began shaking his left arm. He hit the snake with his right hand. Rick jumped out of the car at about the same time Jeff crawled out.

By the time Jeff got around to the other side of the car, Rick was jumping up and down shouting, "Turn me loose!" The snake was still attached to his left hand.

Jeff drew his gun and shouted, "Be still. I'll shoot it."

Surprisingly Rick stood almost like a statue. Jeff shot twice. The second bullet hit the snake, and it dropped.

"Get into the car," Jeff ordered Rick. Jeff turned to Jason and shouted, "Put the snake in your trunk and follow me to the hospital. Look around and see if Debra is near here."

"I'll call ahead to the hospital and get them ready," Jason shouted back. He jumped out with his umbrella and opened up his car trunk. He picked up the snake carefully on the end of his umbrella and threw it into his trunk.

Rick's muscular activity and the increase in his heart action when he had been jumping up and down trying to free himself from the snake had accelerated the speed of venom. Once back in the car Rick looked at the wound on his hand. There were two small punctures about three quarters of an inch apart. Two large drops of a clear serous-like fluid tinged with blood oozed from the two punctures. He did not even bother to look at the wounds on his leg.

There was a burning pain around the wounds on his hand and leg. The pain rapidly increased in intensity and extended in a circular fashion around the wounds.

About fifteen minutes passed before Jeff entered the emergency entrance of St. Joseph's Hospital. Rick was complaining about pains shooting up his leg and arm. "I'm beginning to feel dizzy," cried Rick.

Jeff kept wondering how Debra Sweeney had been able to get into his car without disturbing the tape. She must have seen him putting it on the car door. Now Rick was having to pay! He should have had at least one more safeguard on his car to prevent anyone from entering without his knowledge.

By the time the attendants at the hospital helped Rick from the car, he began to lose control of his leg muscles, and he staggered when left unsupported.

Once in the hospital there was some confusion. No one could initially identify the snake Jason brought into the hospital and flung on the floor. Finally one nurse mentioned that the snake had a hood. "Maybe it's a cobra. I saw a man kiss a cobra at a snake show last year on television."

Finally, a short doctor came into the emergency room. His five-foot-seven-inch height made him hard to spot in a crowd, but he took control. He gave Rick a shot of anti-venom.

About forty minutes after the snakebites, the paralysis of Rick's arms and legs increased. His lower jaw began to fall, and frothy viscid saliva oozed from his mouth. He began to moan, shaking his head from side to side. He spoke as if he were drunk.

Rick's breathing gradually became slower and finally ceased forty minutes after he was bitten. His death occurred forty-two minutes after the infliction of the first bite.

Jeff Burke had cheated death again. But this time fate had taken someone else in his place.

When Jeff got home he was depressed, but a telephone call shifted his attention to another matter. It was Hank Brown.

"Do you remember Rob Fowler?"

"Who could forget him. We couldn't tie him to the Flesher operation. What's he up to?"

"He got busted on a marijuana rap. The cops called me. Rob wants to talk to you and me about trading some information. I'm going to see him at 5:45. 1 know you have been canned, but do you want to be there when I talk to Rob?"

"Yes, I'll be there. Which station?"

"The one on St. Paul Street. I'll see you there."

Jeff was waiting with Hank at the police station to see Rob. "They caught him with about a ton of pot in a horse trailer. The police seized his truck, horse trailer, $4,575 cash and the ton of illegal weed. Apparently, he purchased it at the Mexican border and drove to Baltimore. The way I figure it ..." Hank was interrupted by a policeman leading Rob into the small room.

"Hello, Rob," Hank rose and shook Rob's hand. "This is Jeff Burke."

"Yeah, I know him. You and him caught my old lady at the Flesher plumbing outlet."

Jeff smiled slightly as he remembered Hank putting holes in Rob's condoms at the time they searched his home.

"You guys put me in here," Rob continued. "You cut off my money. They tell me I can get ten years. I don't want to rot in prison. I can give you some important information about a big man in the IRS if you'll help me beat this rap."

"Look, Rob, you have more problems than you think. I made some calculations on the way over here. The way I figure it, you owe taxes on about $137,000."

"What?" Rob looked surprised and stared at Hank.

"This is probably not the first load you've sold. Assume you sold only one other load. You probably grossed $780,000 from the pot sales. Say we allow a deduction of about $482,000 including $280,000 for the cost of the weed, $320,000 sales commissions, and $40,000 of the driver's expense. That leaves a net profit of $337,000."

"Wait a minute, Hank," Jeff interrupted. "For a drug-related business, a taxpayer is only allowed to deduct cost of goods sold."

"Look, guys, that was my first load. I don't owe any taxes. I'm an honest man. I don't need any trouble with you guys. But I can help you. I know some juicy gossip about your fancy Commissioner—Callaway is his name. But you guys have got to help me. Will you?" His voice was unsteady.

Hank's eyes involuntarily swung toward Jeff when Rob mentioned the name Callaway. He leaned forward in his straight chair and said slowly, "How do you know Commissioner Callaway?"

"I know some information about him." Rob looked more confident now. He had seen both Hank and Jeff's sudden interest when he mentioned the name Callaway. "Now can you help me?"

"I am currently working with the supervisor of a special strike force which deals with corruption in the federal government. I believe I can help you if your information is worthwhile." Jeff spoke for the first time.

Rob turned to Jeff and said, "I knew Tish Scarbourg, a girlfriend of Richard Onner. He's an IRS employee. I lived with her before she met Onner."

"Really!" exclaimed Hank.

"So, anyway, Tish worked for this Commissioner Callaway. She broke up with Onner for several months and started fooling with Callaway. She learned that Callaway sometimes employs a hit woman." Rob hesitated to dramatically allow this disclosure to have its full impact on his two listeners.

"Surely Callaway didn't just tell Tish such damaging information," Hank said.

"Apparently, Callaway got drunk or careless one night and called this hit woman from Tish's apartment. Tish overheard him, became jealous of him calling another woman, and threatened to tell his wife about their affair. To pacify her, Callaway told Tish the truth—that the woman was a professional killer."

"How did you find out about this?" asked Hank in a disbelieving tone.

"Tish got into trouble. She got caught with some crack and wound up in jail. She couldn't find Onner, and she called me. I helped her get out of the pokey, and I stayed with her the rest of the weekend. She told me about the incident with the phone.

"Somehow Onner and Callaway got to know one another through Tish. Onner was able to get Callaway to transfer him to Martinsburg, Virginia."

"That's West Virginia," corrected Hank.

"What?"

"Martinsburg is in West Virginia."

"Okay, West Virginia. Tish still lives with Onner in Martinsburg. She calls me every once in a while when she gets mad at Onner."

"Would you testify to this in court?" asked Jeff.

"Sure, if you get me off."

"That's no good, Rob," said Hank. "How do we know you're not making this up to get out of the slammer? Besides, it's hearsay evidence. It's worthless. We have to get this Tish woman. Sorry, Rob."

Hank rose and said, "Come on, Jeff. He's wasting our time."

"Wait a minute," Rob pleaded, obviously scared. "I can help you get Tish. If I get her for you, will you help me?"

"Come on, Rob. You're going to testify that she smoked some pot. That's not going to help us."

"No! That's not it." Rob was squeezing the arms of the chair firmly. "I worked with Tish about five years ago in a confidence game. I'm sure she didn't report any of the income."

"Well, now, Rob. You may have something." Hank's eyebrows lifted as he sat back down in his chair. "Tell me more."

Rob seemed to regain some confidence as he sat more erect in his chair. His deep-set brown eyes flashed at Hank. "I'm involved, so you'll have to get me immunity. Can you? Can you help me beat this drug rap?"

"Rob, we would not be worth our IRS salt if we could not help you," replied Hank.

Rob turned and gave Jeff a quizzical look.

Jeff nodded in agreement.

"She was involved in a Ponzi scheme," Rob began. "She and I both were in Los Angeles then. She was a nurse, and she started going with an intern. I met them both at the same hospital. Due to their expertise and connections in the first aid field, we—they represented to friends, acquaintances, and various relatives that they were able to purchase ambulance shells directly from the factory, equip them, and sell the finished ambulances to municipalities or companies at a substantial profit."

Both Jeff and Hank remained silent.

"The business did not exist. They promised to share the profits with the others if they would loan them money to purchase the original vehicle. Tish—she used another name in L.A.—and Kenneth persuaded a number of investors to advance money to them in return for a 25% interest. They had no intentions to repay the loans. They would promise to repay the investors within one month after their original investment plus the high interest."

Rob paused for a moment and began again. "Over a two-year period they collected about $1.7 million from at least fifty-seven individuals. Throughout this period they gave different investors contradictory stories about the business, including the identity of the customers, from whom they were buying the vehicles, why they did not borrow from conventional financing sources, and why they were unable to repay investors on schedule. They had about twenty different reasons for slow payments, ranging from the need to care for a mentally ill and suicidal sister to the fact that the son of the person who was to deliver the money had been in a motorcycle accident and needed to have his arm amputated."

"What happened?" asked Hank, clearly interested.

"Tish and Kenneth left town. Vanished. Changed their names."

"I don't believe it," Jeff said, eyeing Rob coldly.

"How do you know so much?" Hank asked.

Rob sighed. "I was Kenneth."

An obviously surprised Hank said, "What happened to the money?"

"We went to Las Vegas. Tish got more money than I did. She could hustle better than me. She would promise the suckers that in addition to a return on their investment, they would receive new automobiles free or at special discounts. She would tell them the company was able to obtain these good deals because of the many purchases of ambulances from automobile manufacturers. I lost most of my money gambling in Vegas."

"Does Tish still have her money?" asked Hank.

"Some of it. She didn't gamble as much as I did."

"Rob," said Jeff, "Would Tish meet you — say for lunch? You could tell her you have another deal cooking."

"Sure she would meet me, man. She owes me a lot."

"Arrange it for Saturday. You should be out on bail by then. You'll post bail, won't you, Hank?" Jeff turned to Hank.

"Why not, it's only the IRS's money. My boss loves me — I hope."

Chapter 24

What is the difference between a taxidermist and a tax collector? The taxidermist takes only your skin.

—Mark Twain

Tish Scarbourg was surprised to hear from Rob. She had intentionally tried to suppress that part of her life. She still had some of the money from that stage of her life in a numbered account in Miami. She was skeptical of Rob having any type of productive scheme, except to borrow or milk money from her. Yet she really had no choice; Rob knew where too many of her skeletons were hidden.

When she came into the small restaurant she saw Rob sitting with two men at a corner table. They looked like businessmen. Tish thought that maybe Rob might be after something other than borrowing money.

Tish walked to the table confidently. She was still an attractive woman. Even with the years, she was tall and not overweight. Of course, her blonde hair was not natural, and there were some slight lines in her face. But her figure still made men take a second or third look when she passed by.

Only Rob rose when she reached the table. "Hello, Tish. Glad you could come. Is a Scotch on the rocks okay?"

"Yes, that will be fine."

Rob motioned to a passing waiter and ordered the drink.

There was an uncomfortable silence as they waited for the drink. Finally Rob said, "Tish, these gentlemen are IRS Special Agents. They know about our ambulance scam."

The color drained from her tanned cheeks. She took a perfunctory look at Hank's extended Special Agent Commission. Then she said in a somber voice, "Anyone can have a badge like that. What are you trying to pull, Rob?"

"It's no joke, Tish. They got me on a drug charge. I had no choice. They need you to get your ex-friend, the Commissioner."

"What are you talking about?" Tish tried to sound convincing. There was a sour feeling at the bottom of her stomach.

Hank spoke first. "Ms. Scarbourg, I checked your tax returns this morning on the computer."

"Besides, even if I didn't report it, that was five years ago. The statute of limitations has run out. You can't get me."

"Wrong again, Ms. Scarbourg. There is no statute of limitations in the case of fraud. Suppose you calm down and listen. We are not really after you. We want the Commissioner. If what Rob has told us is correct, you can help us."

"What's in it for me?" She was slowly drumming her fingertips on the tabletop. Her voice was calmer and quieter. She took a sip of the Scotch after the waiter set it in front of her.

When the waiter moved away, Jeff said, "Ms. Scarbourg, the IRS can handle a taxpayer in a whimsical, unpredictable, and highly personal manner. We can easily turn you over to our collection division whose job is to go charging after overdue money. These boys can be high handed and obnoxious."

Jeff raised his right hand and continued, "One revenue collector in my office seized a $3,000 bank account that a taxpayer had set up to pay for his wife's cancer treatment because it was the readiest asset the taxpayer had. Last year a revenue officer seized a guard dog company and sold off his dogs within two days to the taxpayer's competitor before the man had a chance to obtain the money to pay. These guys get points for seizing money from taxpayers on Social Security, on welfare, or from a pension plan. The bottom line: revenue collectors are low lifes."

What Jeff did not mention was that about 12 of these revenue officers per week report threats and about 40 or more are assaulted per year.

Jeff turned to Hank. "Tell her about that Tracy fellow in Montana."

"Ah, yes. Mr. Tracy was a TV personality. He had a talk show and frequently invited tax protesters to his show. It seems that he openly expressed sympathy with a tax protester's statement that the IRS uses illegal methods to collect taxes. Some agents paid a visit to the TV station demanding tape recordings of his past shows. He was fired the next day."

"An unemployed Mr. Tracy wrote and published a booklet entitled 'Guide to Tax Rebellion.' Several months later agents demanded from his bank microfilm records of the names of all the people who paid for copies of the booklet by check. Sales of his book naturally took a nose-dive. But Mr. Tracy was a slow learner. Later he led an anti-tax rally in front of the IRS office in Salt Lake City. Nearly 150 people stood in the pouring rain to protest excessive taxation. An IRS agent stated in public 'The IRS is going to get Sam Tracy.' "

"And they did. Four days later he was taken to the Salt Lake City jail where he was detained for 14 hours without explanation. The next morning Tracy was brought in chains before a U.S. magistrate and charged with illegal possession of an IRS insignia. It seems that Tracy had displayed IRS publication No. 34, the seizure notice, at the protest rally. Any citizen can legally get this notice under the Freedom of Information Act."

"When released from custody, Tracy found that his auto, office, and briefcase had been searched without a warrant. Business funds of $30,000 were missing. He was unable to recover these funds. At his trial for illegal possession of the IRS Insignia, he was denied a jury trial and summarily found guilty by the judge. He received the maximum sentence of six months in jail." Hank stopped talking from sheer loss of breath, but he did smile in self-satisfaction.

Jeff continued. "There was a gentleman in New Jersey who filed tax returns claiming two burros as children. He might have never been caught, but he listed the names of the children as Sassafras and Happyjack. Well ..."

Tish interrupted just as Jeff reached forward and jabbed a finger in mid-air. "Don't give me any more Gestapo stories. I'm impressed. What do you want?"

Hank answered. "Would you tell us about Jimmy Callaway?"

Tish again gave Rob a hard look. "I had a thing going with Jimmy. There's no law against that. That was some time ago."

"Tell us about his hit woman."

There was a short pause, and Tish leaned forward and began. "We were at his house in Maryland. His wife was visiting her folks in North Carolina. I was his mistress and was very possessive. He had been drinking and was in the bathroom when the telephone rang. I answered it, and it was a woman—not his wife. I left the phone off the hook and took him another phone into the bathroom. He has phone plug-ins all over the house. To make a long story short, I went back to the other phone and listened to the conversation."

"The caller was a professional killer. Jimmy made arrangements for her to kill a local politician in North Carolina who was holding up his possible appointment as the Commissioner of the IRS. She asked for $10,000 to be placed in a numbered account in Switzerland. He was to put $10,000 more in the account after the transaction was completed. She used the word 'transaction.'"

"Maybe I put the phone down too soon, but Jimmy seemed to know afterwards that I had listened to the conversation. He got extremely angry. I told him that I had heard very little. He was so mad and angry that I left."

"Why didn't he just have you killed?" asked Hank.

"I thought about that, so I wrote up a summary of the conversation, dated it, and put it with my will in my safe deposit box. I told Jimmy the next day that I was frightened, so I had written up the conversation and had given it to my lawyer to be opened in the case of my untimely death. The whole event seemed to place a chill over our affair, and we broke up several weeks later. Actually, he is the one who introduced me to Richard Onner. I really have not seen him since that time, but I do read about him frequently in the paper. He seems to be doing well."

Jeff excitedly asked, "Did you write down the number of the Swiss bank account?"

"Yes. Initially I thought the information might be worthwhile. But Richard and Jimmy correspond frequently. They apparently are involved in several business projects. Besides, who wants to mess around blackmailing a professional killer."

"Do you know the woman's name?" spoke Hank.

"No, she didn't mention her name or address."

"Do Richard and Jimmy collect rare coins?" asked Jeff.

"Richard does. He gets some crazy junk mail. The other day he got a piece which said Doomsday! Will it be October 15, 2017? They were trying to sell a monthly advisory letter called the 'Uptight Spike.' I don't know about Jimmy. I really don't. I could ask Richard."

"No, don't," exclaimed Jeff. "Could we get the Swiss bank account number from your safe deposit box?"

"What are you going to do to me?" asked Tish.

"Nothing if we can get Jimmy Callaway. You may have to testify sometime in the future. But no one knows about your little ambulance episode. We'll keep it that way if you will cooperate with us. We'll need a copy of your written account of Callaway's phone conversation. Also, you should tell Onner nothing—absolutely nothing."

"I won't say a word. Jimmy would have me killed. I'll take you to get the Swiss account number."

True to her word, Tish did have a Swiss bank account number and a signed statement as to a conversation between Jimmy Callaway and an unknown woman. Jeff and Hank got a copy of the statement, and they went to Hank's office.

In Hank's modest office—if it could be called an office—Jeff said, "We really have little evidence on Debra Sweeney. She's probably not going to help us unless we can get her money from her Swiss safe deposit box. Can we get it?"

"I believe so," said Hank. "There was a court case a number of years ago when an American won the Irish Sweepstakes—a cool 50,000 Irish pounds. About $140,000 then. When he learned he had a silent partner in his winnings—the IRS—he deposited the money into a secret foreign bank on the Island of Jersey, between England and France. Well, the taxpayer was convicted of income tax evasion and went to prison. But his money was still in the foreign bank. The IRS went to court again to repatriate his assets from the foreign bank and deposit the funds with the clerk of the court. We won. The taxpayer's money came back to the U.S. They didn't know his bank account number."

"What section of the law did they use?"

Hank picked up a copy of the Internal Revenue Code of 1986 and flipped through it. "I believe it was Section 7402. Here it is— Section 7402(a)."

Jeff took the dog-eared copy of the Code from Hank and read: "The district courts of the United States at the instance of the United States shall have such jurisdiction to make and issue in civil actions, writs and orders of injunction, and of *ne exeat republica,* orders appointing receivers, and such judgments and decrees as may be necessary or appropriate for the enforcement of the internal revenue laws. The remedies hereby provided are in addition to and not exclusive of any and all other remedies of the United States in such courts or otherwise to enforce such laws."

Jeff shook his head. "It doesn't say anything to me."

"Be more positive, Burke. We have to win. We are the good guys with white hats. We always win, don't we?"

Chapter 25

Due to the sheer size of the IRS, waste and mismanagement occur on a massive scale.
— Rep. Stephen Horn, R-Calif.

Tish Scarbourg quickly accepted a deal to testify against Jimmy Callaway. After all, the immunity from prosecution deal meant that she no longer had to worry about the past coming back to haunt her. She no longer had to worry about jail for her scheme with Rob, nor would she concern herself with ever needing to use the letter she had put in her safe-deposit box. This certainly had been her lucky day.

Unfortunately, neither she nor the IRS agents bothered to notice a woman wearing a brown wig in the corner of the restaurant bent over her cup of coffee during the entire meeting. Nor had any of them noticed the small camera she had cleverly concealed in a book on the table to her left. The woman snapped off a few pictures of the meeting by simply pressing the insignia on the book's cover.

Minutes after they left, the woman received change from the waitress and made her way outside and make a call on her cell phone.

Commissioner Callaway answered his private phone and was greeted by a voice he immediately recognized. He had been anticipating a call from Debra Sweeney for some time, and he did not hesitate to meet her in the park in one hour.

Sitting side by side on a park bench with their back facing a rock wall, Debra Sweeney revealed her day's work. The color drained from the Commissioner's face as he ogled the photographs. The look of surprise was quickly replaced with a cold piercing glare. He seemed to be looking right through Debra.

"Why haven't you taken care of this problem?" he rasped.

"This cat's got nine lives. He should be dead already. But don't worry, his luck is about to run out," reported Debra confidently.

"I'm sorry but that gives me little comfort. Since our deal hasn't been delivered in a timely fashion, the noose around my neck has just gotten tighter. The woman in the picture is Tish Scarbourg. She is not only a threat to me but to you as well."

"I'll take care of it. I will need a little more incentive, however."

Commissioner Callaway countered with a hateful look and replied, "You will get no incentive from me. This mess was created by you. You can clean it up." And the meeting was over.

Later a phone call to the Department of Motor Vehicles provided Debra with Tish's home address. Debra easily picked the lock to Tish's home, and a quick survey of her place gave Debra the perfect idea for Tish's demise.

Tish arrived home several hours later. After showering she went directly to bed, secure in the thought that all the problems of her past would soon be washed away. She felt so relaxed as she lay in her large, luxurious, soft bed. So relaxed in fact, she was asleep within minutes. She didn't even feel the bed move as Debra slithered out from under the bed, only disturbing the flowing dust ruffle, which hung down to the floor concealing her. Likewise, she was just as undisturbed when the hypodermic needle filled with cobra venom slid into her skin.

The following morning the mood in Jeff's apartment was somber. With their star witness gone, Jeff, Hank, and Jason were becoming anxious. Hank also was receiving pressure from his boss because he had bailed out Rob with departmental money, and with Tish dead, the money was spent for nothing. Jeff knew he was running out of time, and Jason figured it was only a matter of time before she realized he was still alive and began her pursuit of him once more. They all looked beat. The well of ideas had dried up, and they could do little to prevent their names from being next in the obituaries.

Jason finally broke the haunting silence with a desperate plea, "What can we do? We have no one to tie Onner, Callaway, Rosenbaum, and Debra Sweeney together. We're sunk!"

Jeff tried to add a little optimism, "Maybe there is. Maybe we can invent someone." Hank and Jason shot blank stares at each other, half-confused and half thrilled that there still was a chance they could survive this ordeal.

"Do tell," prodded Jason.

Jeff flashed Jason a knowing look. "There still is one person who could draw their attention."

Hank was getting eager, "Who?"

"Do you remember Henry Silverman?"

"I thought you made a deal with him? He won't help us," replied Jason.

"We only have a tentative agreement. I didn't make any promises."

"Who's Henry Silverman?" inquired Hank.

"He's the one who started us on Onner's trail," explained Jeff, "He's the one who told Onner how to rip-off the IRS. Now he's the bait."

"Bait!" exclaimed Hank.

"He's the only one who can testify against Onner. Maybe if we get him excited enough he will do something stupid and hang himself."

"What do you need? We're behind you," Hank resolutely proclaimed.

Half an hour later, everyone knew what to do, and Jeff's plan began to unfold. He only hoped it worked. They could be in serious trouble if it failed.

Disguised, Jason exited via the back door. After getting into his car, he drove directly to the home of one of his close friends who just happened to be a local judge. An hour later he was at the residence of Richard Onner. Luckily, Onner was away for the time being on another coin buying spree. With the proper authorization, once inside Jason bugged all of Onner's phones. He then sat in his car across the street with his listening equipment and waited for Onner to return home.

Jeff immediately dialed the phone number of Henry Silverman. Henry was less than pleased to find out he wasn't out of the woods yet. He reluctantly agreed to participate in the plan, since any risk was worth taking if it meant he wouldn't have to go back to jail. Plus it sounded as if Jeff had all his bases covered in his plan.

As soon as Jeff hung up, Hank was out of the door. He was an acquaintance of Attorney General Ben Gibson. They had both attended the University of Alabama and they had met at an alumni fundraising dinner where they had shared a table together.

The Attorney General owned a three-story mansion, with a tennis court, swimming pool, and three-car garage. Hank hesitated to push the call button outside the gate for fear he might smudge it.

A guard's static voice came back over the speaker after a few moments. "What's your name and purpose for being here."

Hank's confident reply was, "I'm here to see Attorney General Gibson. My name is Hank Brown. I'm an old friend of his from Alabama."

"Make an appointment and come back later," was the guard's blunt response.

"Look, I'm Hank Brown. I'm an IRS agent, and it is imperative that I speak with him at once."

"One moment, Mr. Brown. He may have a minute to speak with you."

A few minutes later Hank got the positive answer "You may proceed up the drive, Mr. Brown." A second later the gates began to open. The landscaping was breathtaking. Lining the drive were large century old oak trees. Their long branches created a canopy over the drive. Flowers of all the colors of the rainbow sprung up in patches out on the lawn. As he took in the scenery he couldn't help notice security cameras strategically mounted on tree limbs or atop small metal poles. Standing in the doorway with the broad smile of a typical politician was Attorney General Gibson.

Ben greeted him with a firm handshake, a big smile, and a pleasant, "Hank Brown, long time no see. To what do I owe this pleasure?"

Hank was rather astonished that Ben had recognized him; after all, they had only met once. "I'm surprised you remembered me. I figured you had forgotten about the dinner we attended together."

"Of course not, Hank. Of course, I remember the dinner. Come inside."

The interior of the house was just as breathtaking as the outside. Two wide staircases circled up to the second story, and two security guards stood beneath a large teardrop chandelier, which dangled over the foyer. Large oil paintings decorated the walls. Hank guessed they were of Ben's ancestors. "Nice place!"

"Yeah, I take great pleasure in the finer things in life," replied Ben rather immodestly as he led Hank to the study off to the right.

Hank plopped down in a large plush armchair as Ben closed the door behind them. Ben circled around behind his desk. "What can I do for you, Hank? I'm sorry I don't have more time to catch up with what has been going on in your life, but I have a meeting in a few minutes. But nothing is so important that I can't spare a few minutes for an old friend."

"Well," started Hank, "to get to the point, a couple of agents and I believe there is an elaborate scheme involving a few IRS agents, a man named Richard Onner, a millionaire named Rosenbaum, a hit woman named Debra Sweeney, and Commissioner Callaway. Together they are extorting millions of dollars a year from the government, and ..."

"Wait, wait, wait," exclaimed Ben "What are you talking about? Jimmy? He's a good friend of mine. I find this a little hard to swallow. These are some very serious accusations, Hank. Do you have any evidence to support your claims? If you are right, this is something serious."

"We do have evidence. Jeff Burke and Jason Pabst, the other two agents I'm working with, uncovered the scheme and have enough evidence to convict Rosenbaum and Onner. We have devised a plan to catch Debra Sweeney and Commissioner Callaway. You will probably receive a letter in the mail sometime soon in regards to all these details, but this couldn't wait. We all fear for our lives, and we need to act fast."

"Really?" inquired Ben.

"Yes. That's why I'm here. I was hoping that you would assist us in tapping the Commissioner's phone."

"Maybe. How's the plan supposed to work?"

"Simple. We were able to get the cooperation of a tax fraud specialist named Henry Silverman. He was contacted by Onner regarding ideas as to how to hide the extorted money he's received. Henry will contact Onner and give the impression he is going to extort outrageous amounts of money from him and arrange to meet him in a restaurant. Onner won't be able to pay, and in turn he will contact the Commissioner. That's why we need your help in bugging the Commissioner's phone. Jimmy knows he can't afford to lose Onner, so he will contact the hit woman, Debra Sweeney, who is already in town, to eliminate Silverman. He isn't a dumb man, so he most likely will want to meet her in another location. We need the bug so we can photograph them together to establish a link between him and the hit woman."

"I see. Then you will apprehend her before she makes the hit on Henry."

"Correct," answered Hank triumphantly. He apparently had sold Ben on the idea. This whole ordeal would soon be over.

"I'm so glad you came to see me with this," said Ben with the same wolfish smile on his face as he rose from his chair. "I am sorry to hear about Jimmy. He's a good friend of mine, but no one is above the law. If he's doing something wrong, then he should be punished. I'm also sorry to hear about Jack Rosenbaum. You see, I've also become a collector of rare coins," pointing to a glass case sitting on a bookshelf. "They are some of my most prized possessions."

Something was bothering Hank, but he wasn't sure what it was. He dismissed the idea and gave Ben a firm handshake, "I'm glad to have your help. I owe you one."

"No problem. I hope that the guard wasn't rude to you," said Ben apologetically.

Hank waved off Ben's apology. "Not at all. I know they have a job to do."

"I don't know if you noticed the security cameras or not. The guards are particularly suspicious of new faces that carry guns. It's their job. That's a real nice gun, by the way. What kind is it?" inquired Ben, pointing to the gun tucked in Hank's belt.

"A .357 colt python," replied Hank.

"I like guns, also. Can I see it?"

Hank smiled proudly as he pulled it out to give Ben a closer look.

"No! No! Don't shoot me! Please don't kill me!" shrieked Ben hysterically as he backed against his desk.

Hank still had the gun outstretched with the butt pointed toward Ben when it finally clicked. He felt so stupid. He was too preoccupied with getting the permission of Ben to ever think whether or not he was somehow involved. Why hadn't he caught on sooner?

Hank's body crumpled to the ground, when the security guards charged into the room and riddled his body with bullets. His hand was still gripping the barrel.

Attorney General Gibson walked calmly over to Hank's body lying in a growing pool of blood, the wolfish smile returning to his face. He removed the gun from Hank's hand with Kleenex, wiped the barrel clean, and then replaced it in Hank's hand, this time wrapping Hank's fingers around the butt. Gibson said out loud, "As Bill Clinton said, I feel your pain."

He returned to his desk, once again changing his demeanor as he dialed 911, "Help! There's a man here with a gun! Hurry!"

The smile returned to his face once again as he cradled the receiver. He motioned for his guards to leave, and he then picked it up again. This time he dialed the private number of Jimmy Callaway.

After being informed by Ben, without hesitation Callaway paged two people. Richard Onner returned his phone call almost immediately.

"Richard, I was wondering if you could meet me for lunch, if you aren't too busy."

Richard was perplexed, "Lunch! What about ... ?"

"Oh, come on Richard. It won't take long. Just a cup of coffee at the place next to that florist where you always go. One hour."

"Ok," was Richard's puzzled reply.

Another phone rang again moments later. The other end was silent. "Coffee and Company, half an hour," ordered the Commissioner. Then the line went dead.

Half an hour later Jimmy Callaway entered a small specialty coffee shop. He recognized the woman sitting in the corner and sat down beside her. Debra was dressed in her usual disguise, a brown wig and large sunglasses. She didn't raise her eyes from her coffee as he sat.

Jimmy leaned over the table so their faces were just inches apart, "Two more to go."

"Who?"

"Jeff Burke." She cringed at the sound of his name and the thought of how he had continually eluded her. " ... and Jason Pabst."

"The Pabst job is done," rasped Debra. Jimmy's sole reply was a scornful stare, and she knew she had somehow been tricked.

"Jason is still alive. I suggest you watch from the bookstore across the street. One of them—Jason or Jeff—is sure to show up in the next half-hour. The other will be at Jeff's apartment waiting for a phone call." Jimmy was furious. He never would have had this problem if she had done the job right in the first place. "Do it right this time. No more mistakes or you will wish you would have chosen another line of work."

Debra was steaming. She had been tricked and was being made a fool. Even if she completed the job right this time, her business might still suffer. She had been sloppy. Enraged she stalked out of the coffee shop to the bookstore where she occupied herself with a copy of a model airplane magazine as she waited.

Onner arrived shortly thereafter. She observed him enter the shop and sit with the Commissioner. She also recognized Jason Pabst through his pathetic disguise and immediately moved in for the kill. As she made her way across the street she took out the blowgun fashioned like a lipstick tube. Shielding her face with a make-up compact she entered the shop a few steps behind Jason, and took a seat directly behind Jason. A twist of the lipstick tube exposed the hollow barrel of the blowgun, and she blew the dart precisely into Jason's neck.

Jason's muscles tightened briefly before he convulsed, then collapsed at the table. Before his head hit the table, she snatched the dart from his neck and headed for the car. Destination, Jeff Burke's apartment.

Through the window she could see Jeff pacing back and forth as she pulled up. He was visibly troubled. No more games; no more clever tricks. She had had it with Jeff Burke; she was tired of messing with him. She was talking under her breath as she fastened a silencer on the tip of her Glock 9. She proceeded directly up the stairs to the front door of his apartment and rang the bell.

Jeff was startled by the sudden noise. He knew it had to be trouble since neither Hank nor Jason had contacted him since this morning.

He pulled out his revolver and cautiously approached the door. He stood off to the side of the door and cried, "Who is it?"

After a few seconds of not hearing a reply, he cautiously leaned over and peered through the peephole, half-wondering if it was just a kid playing a "ring and run" prank. When he looked out the peephole and only saw black he knew he had made a fatal mistake. He didn't even see the bullet as it came through the peephole.

Good doesn't triumph over evil every time.

For good measure, Debra sprayed three more bullets through the door.

Epilogue

The world is not the way they tell you it is.
　　　　　　—Adam Smith, in "The Money Game"

Two weeks later, the Pikeville local newspaper carried the following electrifying front-page headline on Wednesday: "Minister's Wife Jailed." The copyrighted story began as follows: "A mother of two, Debra Sweeney, is an alleged professional killer. Wife of a Baptist minister, her apparent idiosyncrasy was a passion for exotic 'hits' of her intended victims. Bombings, poison darts, and a cobra bite were only some of the techniques used by this mother and writer of children's books. She is apparently connected to a much wider 'Neutrongate' fraud that may involve the U.S. Treasury Department. Her bond has been set at $750,000. Reverend John Sweeney was unavailable for comment."

* * *

"Fox News" broke the story last night when an unidentified IRS agent spoke about his narrow escape from death. Apparently one agent, Nick Anderson, was allegedly killed by a flying model airplane in Washington, D. C., last month, and another Washington detective, Rick Garrison, was killed by the bite of an exotic cobra several days ago.

* * *

On Thursday, the *Arizona Republic* carried this headline. "$758 Million Tax Liens Hit Phoenix Tycoon." The front page story ran as follows: "Alleged nonpayment of $758 million in income taxes has prompted federal action against Jack Rosenbaum, Phoenix businessman and personal friend of IRS Commissioner Jimmy Callaway, officials said here."

"Federal tax liens were placed against Rosenbaum's personal assets as well as his financial empire, which includes more than 1,500 coin shops throughout the country along with the world's largest mail-order coin business located in Phoenix, the Internal Revenue Service said this morning."

"Rosenbaum also controls the Rosenbaum Ammunition Plant located near Vulture Mine. The federal official indicated that much of the unpaid taxes had been used to develop a neutron bomb, which has been outlawed for many years. The scam is apparently worse than the Iran-Contra affair in the eighties."

"The liens were filed with the recorder's offices in 1,570 counties where Rosenbaum owns property. This action served notice to persons doing business with Rosenbaum in any of the counties in which the IRS has a 'prior claim on any assets' owned by Rosenbaum, the spokesman said."

"The liens were filed at the same time IRS agents served Rosenbaum's attorney, Mark White, with a 'jeopardy assessment,' which the spokesman said was a harsh action. There is no notice. You pay up now."

"The spokesman said that the IRS resorts to the procedure only when the taxpayer is preparing to leave the country or go into hiding, or if the taxpayer is going to place his assets beyond government reach, or if the taxpayer's financial solvency is or appears to be imperiled."

"Rosenbaum has the 'judicial right to appeal within ninety days' the jeopardy assessment in federal civil court, the spokesman continued."

"The liens represent one of the largest income tax claims since the income tax law became effective in March, 1913. The spokesman would not say how Rosenbaum could have incurred such a huge tax liability. But other sources indicate that some well-placed IRS employees were involved in this gigantic rip-off."

"Rosenbaum reportedly raised two million dollars for President Keeney's political campaigns. The financier was not available for comment at his home in Scottsdale. A spokesman for President Keeney indicated that the President had 'no comment.'"

* * *

On Friday, the *Arizona Republic* carried the follow-up story on page one. "Phoenix businessman Jack Rosenbaum assailed the Internal Revenue Service Thursday for a $758 million income tax lien filed against him and his empire."

"The fifty-five-year-old tycoon issued a statement saying that the lien is 'the most shocking display of bureaucratic power and arrogance I've ever seen leveled against an individual citizen of the United States.'"

"At some bureaucratic levels I am being attacked as a friend of President Keeney. It appears to me that some governmental zealots are anxious to develop a little Coingate in Phoenix," he added.

"I am, therefore, determined to take whatever steps are necessary to clear my name from these misleading and contrived actions by certain agencies of the government," Rosenbaum pledged.

* * *

Richard Onner was arrested for tax fraud on a personal level. When it became apparent that Rosenbaum or Callaway would not help him, Onner told of his special assignment by the IRS Commissioner which allowed him to protect Rosenbaum Company by the consolidated tax return computer scheme. Onner spent three years in jail.

* * *

Debra Sweeney was confined for psychiatric observation after providing powers of attorney to information concerning her Swiss bank account. Some of the funds going into this account were traced to Callaway's personal secretary. Neutron Activation Analysis indicated that certain materials found in Debra's workshop were similar to pieces from the model plane which exploded and killed Revenue Agent Nick Anderson. Debra confessed and agreed to testify against Commissioner Callaway to avoid the death penalty. She would have been only the fourth woman to be executed in many years. There was a slight movement in the U.S. to give women equal rights with respect to the death penalty.

* * *

Rob Fowler received a suspended sentence.

* * *

A combination of publicity concerning the Rosenbaum tax fraud with his close association with Callaway and of publicity concerning the hit woman paid by Callaway's personal secretary almost caused a Senate investigation. Callaway quietly resigned several weeks after this publicity and the Senate Committee never met. He went back to North Carolina and practiced law for five years. Then he ran for and was elected to the North Carolina House of Representatives.

* * *

Rosenbaum Company was prosecuted for back taxes only, and paid the largest assessment for back taxes in U.S. history. Defense Department and CIA intervention at the presidential level caused the new IRS Commissioner to quash any criminal proceedings against Jack Rosenbaum. The Federal government quietly confiscated and destroyed a number of primitive neutron bombs found at the Rosenbaum Ammunition Plant.

* * *

Yvonne Talbert became a Special Agent and member of Operation Greenback, a joint effort between the IRS and Customs Special Agents. The sole purpose of Operation Greenback was to investigate Currency Transaction Reports (CTR) and Currency or Monetary Instruments (CMIR) violations. Special Agents are part of thirteen task forces around the nation with the sole purpose of stopping the sale of narcotics.

* * *

Jeff Burke was saved by the bulletproof door, which he had installed two years earlier. Luckily the peephole was bulletproof, also. The three bullets did not get through the door itself.

The bullet shot through the peephole did destroy Jeff's right eye. Not the bullet, but the backward force of the peephole itself destroyed his eye and knocked him unconscious for about 11 minutes.

Jeff Burke wondered how many other companies Onner was helping to cheat the government. Jeff also wondered if there were other computer operators who were doing the same thing. He never found out. Newspaper articles began appearing such as "IRS Horror Stories Prompt Hearings on Proposed Taxpayers' 'Bill of Rights.'" An Arkansas Senator said:

> Like a bully, the IRS relies on intimidation and arm twisting to strike fear into the hearts of those it bullies.... And they do this in the name of compliance. It is my guess that compliance could be improved not by continuing to browbeat taxpayers, but by reestablishing respect for the IRS in the manner in which it performs a difficult and unpopular task.

Former IRS employee John Smith testified in Congress:

> There are a lot of outrageous and arbitrary actions by agents because of the 'unchecked power' of the IRS. Contrary to claims from the National Office, IRS field employees are pressured to produce statistics that show that they are doing their jobs. As the joke in the office used to go: the name of the game is quality. Lots and lots of quality. The IRS equates increased production and increased seizures with increased quality.

Later, Smith admitted that:

> Between 90 and 95 percent of all cases are handled properly by the Service. Given the broad scope of the IRS's mission, this error factor should be considered 'perfect.' What is needed is 'some vehicle where the ordinary person can go' when he experiences unnecessary harassment or illegalities by a revenue or collection agent.

President Keeney asked for and the Democrat-controlled Congress passed a "Taxpayer's Bill of Rights." Internal Security Inspectors could only investigate dishonesty of IRS employees and not other governmental employees.

Within six months Jeff Burke was transferred "temporarily" to the Bureau of Alcohol, Tobacco, and Firearms. Two years later as an ATF agent he was shot in the leg while trying to arrest two buttleggers in New Jersey. The two were involved in contraband cigarette smuggling.

Jeff continued to pitch softball with one eye and a black eye patch. He only wore the eye patch while he pitched softball to confuse and distract the batters. Several umpires tried to force him to remove the eye patch while he pitched under the rule that a pitcher could not wear anything that would confuse or distract the batter. Early in the game he would throw a fast pitch close to or actually hit a batter. Although Jeff did not get all of his strikes called strikes, he never had to remove the black patch to show his glass eye.

* * *

Carl Strovee fled to Caracas, Venezuela, and did not return to the United States until eight years later—under another identity.

* * *

Henry Silverman found a good lawyer and beat his indictment. He moved to New York City and lost in a controversial campaign to become mayor of New York City.

* * *

Attorney General Ben Gibson was never implicated in the death of Hank Brown.

Other Books by Larry Crumbley

- *Trap Doors and Trojan Horses: An Auditing Action Adventure,* Carolina Academic Press, 919-489-7486; Fax 919-493-5668. $25.00.
- *The Big R: A Forensic Accounting Action Adventure,* Carolina Academic Press, 919-489-7486; Fax 919-493-5668. $25.00.
- *Deadly Art Puzzle: Accounting for Murder* (advanced accounting), Thomson Corp., 800-355-9983; Fax 800-487-8488; In Europe, Tel: 44-207-0672500 (UK). $21.95.
- *Simon the Incredible* (finance), Thomson Corp., 800-355-9983; Fax 800-487-8488; In Europe, Tel: 44-207-0672500 (UK). $24.95.
- *The Bottom Line is Betrayal* (general business), Thomson Corp., 800-355-9983; Fax 800-487-8488; In Europe, Tel: 44-207-0672500 (UK). $23.95.
- *Costly Reflections in a Midas Mirror* (cost/managerial accounting), Carolina Academic Press, 919-489-7486; Fax 919-493-5668. $25.00.
- *Accosting the Golden Spire* (basic accounting), Carolina Academic Press, 919-489-7486; Fax 919-493-5668.
- *Dangerous Hoops: A Forensic Marketing Action Adventure,* Baton Rouge: LSU Press, 2011.
- *Computer Encryption in Whispering Caves* (accounting information systems), Cengage Corporation, Philip.Krabbe@cengage.com.
- *Chemistry in Whispering Caves* (Chemistry), Thomson Corp., 800-355-9983; Fax 800-487-8488; In Europe, Tel: 44-207-0672500 (UK), 1998, $24.95.

- *Nonprofit Sleuths: Follow the Money* (governmental accounting), Thomson Corp., 800-355-9983; Fax 800-487-8488; In Europe, Tel: 44-207-0672500 (UK), 1997, $24.95.
- *Greenspan, Burmese Caper* (finance), 2Many Books, 1402 Applewood Road, Baton Rouge, LA 70808, 225-763-6409. Email: twomanybooks@rocketmail.com.

Called a "cross between Mickey Spillane and Mr. Chips" by *The Washington Post*, Dr. Larry Crumbley, CPA, CFF (a.k.a Iris Weil Collett) is the author of twelve other widely adopted novels. *Business Week* in June 1989 called him a mover and shaker, and said he "aims to lend excitement to the study of debits and credits by couching the stuff in romantic prose." With his use of forensic accountants as his major characters, a *New Accountant* article called Crumbley the Mark Twain of the accounting profession. His goal is to spice up ho-hum subjects and to make students think that the accounting profession is much better than the stereotype image they have. According to the *Wall Street Journal,* his novels prove the phrase "suspenseful accounting is not necessarily an oxymoron."

Fortune, June 29, 1991, quoted Crumbley: "to be a good accountant, you have to be a good detective" and called his latest novel an "instructional thriller." Crumbley appeared on the front cover of the December 1988 issue of *Management Accounting* as a bespectacled Mickey Spillane. Kathy Williams, author of *The Case of the Purloined Pagoda* has said to "move over Arthur Hailey." *WG&L Accounting News* compared Crumbley to Indiana Jones. The sometime fedora-donned Crumbley in trench coat could be the John D. MacDonald in the accounting arena with thirteen novels under his belt.